Changing Roles for a New Psychotherapy

Psychotherapy is not a "one size fits all approach." As author John G. Miller describes in *Changing Roles for a New Psychotherapy*, all theoretical orientations have their uses and merits in different situations, and with different clients. Through a varied personal life and professional career, in which he developed a creative psychotherapeutic approach that allows the adaptation of diverse roles with clients, Dr. Miller has gained insights through working in academia, the sciences, management consulting, and a state hospital. He applies these insights, along with those he gained working various summer jobs, to take readers beyond the standard medical model of diagnosis and treatment by drawing on the roles of other professionals. He examines 11 different occupations and explores how the insights gained in each field can enhance therapeutic possibilities. How does cooking relate to psychotherapy? Can accounting change the way psychotherapy is performed? Read on to find out!

John G. Miller, PhD, is Professor Emeritus at the University of Illinois Springfield, and maintains a psychotherapy practice treating adults, adolescents, and families.

Changing Roles for a New Psychotherapy

John G. Miller

Routledge
Taylor & Francis Group
NEW YORK AND LONDON

First published 2013
by Routledge
711 Third Avenue, New York, NY 10017

Simultaneously published in the UK
by Routledge
27 Church Road, Hove, East Sussex BN3 2FA

Routledge is an imprint of the Taylor & Francis Group, an informa business

Library of Congress Cataloging in Publication Data
Miller, John G., 1928–
Changing roles for a new psychotherapy / John G. Miller.
pages cm
Includes bibliographical references and index.
ISBN 978-0-415-89843-0 (hardback : acid-free paper) — ISBN 978-0-415-65657-3 (paperback : acid-free paper)
1. Psychotherapy—Practice. I. Title.
RC465.5.M555 2012
616.89'14068—dc23
2012025683

ISBN: 978-0-415-89843-0 (hbk)
ISBN: 978-0-415-65657-3 (pbk)
ISBN: 978-0-203-07769-6 (ebk)

Typeset in Sabon
by EvS Communication Networx, Inc.

Contents

Acknowledgments

This book was written over a period of time with inputs from my clients, my professors, and academic colleagues at the University of Illinois Springfield and the psychotherapy practice founded by my wife and me in 1978.

For this book I am especially indebted to my wife Kibber, who was my consultant as she typed the first few drafts of this book. Help, guidance, and support came from my brother Dick, who followed me into graduate school and became perhaps a more skilled clinician than I am.

All of my children have also been instrumental in guiding my thoughts and feelings about how to help others. Three of my girls, Nancy, Lisa and Mary have been especially helpful and constructive throughout the drafts of this book.

For the actual production of this book, I thank Linda Lenzini, who translated the notes and concepts from my clinical experiences into its present readable form. Also of invaluable help was my editor, JoAnn Miller, who took the book from a rough manuscript and helped shape it into a book.

Introduction

Becoming a Psychotherapist

During summer breaks, as an undergraduate back in the fifties, I worked as a brush cutter on a state highway survey crew, high in the hills of West Virginia. It was the humblest and dirtiest job on the crew; it required that I forge ahead and cut brush away from the surveyor's line of sight. One day, the head of the crew sent me half a mile ahead, with instructions not to go too near the working stills sometimes found behind barns. His actual words were, "When you go out there, don't go too near the barns, and remember—you don't see or smell the stills behind them."

Years later, memories of those long, hot days as part of the survey crew came back to me as I began my work as a psychotherapist. Just as I had to do as a brush cutter, I had to look past certain things to do my job.

I began to think about other jobs I had had before I became a psychotherapist: painting fences one summer in all kinds of weather, spilling paint, toiling for long days, and persevering until the many yards of fence were painted. I also spent a couple of summers as a welder's helper in a gigantic chemical plant. My job was to haul the master welder's equipment around—torches, tanks, electrical gear—for arc welding. My boss was an artisan, and in addition to watching him work, I had the pleasure of listening as he dispensed advice. I listened carefully, and watched him manage, in what seemed to my young eyes a magical way, to fix anything that came across his path. After earning my degree, I became a chemist, living in Salt Lake City and analyzing uranium ore, which was being mined in Utah. When I was in graduate school earning my doctorate, I worked on an Air Force research contract. Our mission was to design special maps that would help observer bombardiers locate their positions.

I never imagined that any of these experiences would guide me in my career as a psychotherapist. But during my years of teaching psychology and practicing therapy and counseling, I have discovered that I have integrated what I learned from these early roles—painter, brush cutter, welder's assistant, map maker—into my psychotherapeutic approach.

When I began graduate school in 1951, I assumed that what I would learn about psychology would come from my professors and the assigned reading, much of it written by authorities in the field. I was introduced to the work of one of the key leaders in humanistic psychology, Carl Rogers, as part of my required reading. As a graduate assistant, I also got hands-on experience in the classroom with undergraduate students. I embraced Rogers's nondirective approach and the warm, nonjudgmental attitudes that went with it. Like much therapy then, this approach was grounded in the feel-good, human-potential movement of the 1950s and early 1960s. My appreciation for Rogers and my fascination with his nondirective therapy continued as I went on to adapt much of his work with students at the University of Missouri Counseling Bureau several years later.

As a beginning therapist I was entirely caught up in Rogers's approach until I realized that his nondirectional style was not always helpful to students who lacked direction themselves. "Wait a minute," I thought. "I'm trying to use a nondirectional approach with students who have no direction to begin with!" Many of the young people I worked with were drifting along, and I wasn't helping them change that lack of direction.

I then began reading the work of Albert Ellis, who had developed the concept of rational-emotive therapy (RET). Ellis's approach was directed, goal-oriented, and action-driven. It reminded me of the time I had spent designing maps on that Air Force research grant. Like the map drawing, Ellis's approach provided distinct, identifiable targets. For the students I was working with, this meant more emphasis on goals. Later in this book, you will see how mapping, charting, and navigation have continued to influence my practice.

I don't mean to suggest that I abandoned one approach for another. But I did realize that where Rogers's methods provided permissive warmth, Ellis's, while lacking that, gave me a means to control therapeutic encounters and to measure their effectiveness. These qualities were both essential for a young therapist and his clients. Later in this book, I'll discuss in more detail the perception that support and warmth, qualities long valued in therapy, are key to therapeutic success. And I will explain how I learned they are only part of the puzzle.

My therapeutic approach became more integrated in 1959 when I was appointed Director of Counseling and Rehabilitation at a State Hospital in Fulton, Missouri. I saw an opportunity to work with severely ill, institutionalized clients. I knew that this experience would be very valuable. While I was at the State Hospital, the administration instituted a group therapy program, based in part on the work of the psychiatrist Jacob Moreno. Moreno had become world famous as the developer of psychodrama, a powerful way to work with clients in groups. He had been using psychodrama for nearly 40 years, having first introduced group psychotherapy to the American Psychiatric Association in 1932.

I found Moreno's work—which uses role-playing and spontaneous dramatization to guide clients toward insight and change—so creative and effective that I trained at his institutes in Beacon, New York and New York City. As you will see in Chapter 8, "The Psychotherapist as Music Teacher," I put Moreno's ideas to good use at the Missouri State Hospital and other inpatient programs. Creating scenarios that clients will have to face in life in a safe simulated setting is often beneficial. It allows clients to experience stressful circumstances with the support and security of treatment staff. I continued to apply psychodramatic techniques throughout my tenure at the State Hospital.

I completed my doctoral studies in 1966, while working as a psychotherapist at a community mental health center in Burlington, Vermont. Many of my clients were schoolchildren, and a great deal of my time and effort was spent doing testing and assessments, so there were limited opportunities for using psychodrama. It was during this time that I became aware that many of the problems children experienced in school were related to the family dynamics in their homes.

I began reading about family therapy, in particular, the work of therapist Jay Haley. Haley's highly original approach was based on the discoveries of Milton Erickson, one of the most influential therapists of the 20th century. Milton Erickson specialized in medical hypnosis and family therapy and championed the theory of the unconscious mind as creative and solution-generating. He is recognized today for his influence on brief therapy, strategic family therapy, family systems therapy, solution focused brief therapy, and neurolinguistic programming.

Later I was to have an opportunity to train with Haley at his Family Therapy Institute in Washington, DC. I wrote him a letter and asked whether I could be part of the Institute. He wrote back almost immediately, and I began a 2-year internship with him and Chloe Madanes, to whom he was then married. Once a month I would kiss my wife and five children goodbye and fly off for the day, returning late that night. By this time, Jay had moved beyond his earlier problem-solving approach to a more strategic approach. I found his supervision, and that of Chloe Madanes, to be highly effective. Their approach was goal-oriented and highly supportive, and much of what I learned at the Institute is incorporated into my practice to this day. You will particularly find their approach of "turning up the heat" in a case in Chapter 7, "The Psychotherapist as Master Chef."

In graduate school, I had a friend who was a management psychologist. I stayed in touch with him after graduation and learned that he had become a significant force in settings very different from the inpatient facilities and community clinics I had worked in. I was intrigued, and when I had an offer to work in a firm that, like his, was an international management psychology company, I jumped at the chance. I began working at the San Francisco office of Rohrer, Hibler and Replogle.

I had to learn very quickly how our clients' organizations were structured, what kinds of stressors were inherent in that structure, and how the men and women working in those companies were impacted by those stressors. It was in this setting that I met famed transactional analyst Eric Berne. My boss asked me to invite Berne, who ran a training institute in San Francisco, to speak to members of senior management at Rohrer, Hibler and Replogle's customers' firms. Berne was not interested, although the firm was willing to pay a substantial fee. He told me that he didn't do speaking presentations. Instead, he invited me to his San Francisco seminars, where he trained psychiatrists, psychologists, and especially psychotherapists in transactional analysis.

I was able to apply what I learned at Berne's seminars to the work I was doing for the firm. The transactional nature of Berne's approach was one that company managers and key employees understood. He consistently directed attention to those actions which encouraged positive production interaction and compared and contrasted them with destructive behaviors, which he called "games." Berne's best-selling book, *Games People Play*, was familiar in corporate circles at that time. His well-known theories provided common ground for my clients and me. You will see the influence of Berne's theories and my training with him throughout this book, and particularly in Chapter 4, "The Psychotherapist as Banker."

During my years at the management firm I was able to create an intersection for psychodrama and transactional analysis. A racially charged riot had broken out at a San Francisco high school. Eric Berne was asked to help, but he invited me to go in his place. Backed by others from his seminar, I presented to the student body programs that incorporated psychodrama, group therapy, and transactional analysis. That was the end of the violence at that school, which demonstrates that an integrated approach can be effective.

My experience in management consulting is further demonstrated in Chapter 10, "The Psychotherapist as Advertising Executive," where I describe how I used the concept of rebranding to help a client company resolve a critical personnel problem, benefitting both the employees and the company itself.

In 1971, I was offered a position at a brand new university in Springfield, Illinois. The offer came out of the blue, and the job gave me an opportunity to both teach and counsel students. I began expanding my background by reading about psychotherapy research, including the important work of psychologists Allen Bergin and Hans Strupp (e.g., 1955; Strupp, Hadley, & Gomes-Schwartz, 1979) and psychiatrist Aaron Beck (e.g., 1967, 1976; Beck, Ward, Mendelson, Mock, & Erbaugh 1961). These research groundbreakers were establishing protocols for measuring and validating the effects of different kinds of therapy—thus offering therapists an empirical base for their practice. This so-called outcome research was in its infancy in those years and I was eager to know more about it. I continue to be convinced that the development of empirical bases will shape the psychotherapy practice of the future, and I talk about what this future might look like in Chapter 12, "The Psychotherapist as Research Psychologist," and in the Conclusion of this book.

The university, Sangamon State University, later became the University of Illinois-Springfield, and I continued to counsel and teach there while establishing a private psychotherapy practice with my wife, also a therapist. The university offered a terrific learning community, and the city of Springfield was a great place to raise our children.

It was during this time that I began studying the work of Michael White, an Australian social worker and family therapist (e.g., White, 1995; White & Epston, 1990). White is known as the founder of narrative therapy, and reading his work provided me with rich case material that I incorporated into my teaching and my private practice. White drew on psychologist Ted Sarbin's approaches to the narrative nature of human life and crafted it into a psychotherapeutic approach (e.g., Sarbin, 1986). White was a new voice, with valuable case material and important therapeutic insights. I became energized by his theories, and applied many of his discoveries in my classes and in my sessions with clients. Narrative therapy is featured prominently in Chapter 3, "The Psychotherapist as Editor." There I describe several cases where I applied White's techniques, showing how clients can reexamine and rewrite the stories of their lives.

I also had an opportunity to study with Michael White before he died in 2008, at age 60. This book honors him and his innovative approach to therapy, but it is less about rules for *practicing* psychotherapy and more about ways to *think* about psychotherapy. New ways of thinking about psychotherapy are abundant in this book and are illustrated in numerous clinical stories. In Chapter 5, "The Psychotherapist as Artist," for example, I show how a change in perspective guides clients to resolution, and in Chapter 10, "The Psychotherapist as Advertising Executive," I reveal how thinking outside the traditional therapeutic box led to change in an entire corporation.

Some of the roles I describe have not been as fully utilized by the field as they might be. For example, mapping and charting progress, despite its proven utility and demonstrated enhancement for both therapist and client, are not used as frequently as I would like. In Chapter 2, "The Psychotherapist as Navigator," I discuss the value of mapping and tracking progress more fully. Journaling, which is a powerful tool for helping clients retell their own stories, is also underused. In Chapter 12, "The Psychotherapist as Research Psychologist," I talk in more detail about how measurement and research can add credibility to the psychotherapeutic process.

This book continues the quest I began many years ago to develop a creative approach to psychotherapy that allows the adaptation of diverse roles with clients. My sincere desire has always been to expand and energize my own practice with clients, and to offer practical illustrations of these diverse roles and to encourage readers to discover new roles of their own, both within the psychotherapeutic encounter and beyond it, that will help transform their lives and the lives of their clients.

1 Discovering New Roles for Psychotherapists

Early in my practice, it became evident that my clients would reveal what they needed, if I would just let them. Even though I had received extensive training, I realized some of the most powerful lessons were those that came out of my work with clients. The cases in this chapter demonstrate shifts from the standard role of psychotherapist to roles that were unconventional. In each case, the role I adapted was dictated by the unique needs of the client.

Case 1: Margaret

Margaret's first words to me on the telephone were, "I'm desperate! I can't stand the thought of going through another pregnancy like the last one." She had been referred by a friend, whom I had treated for a flying phobia.

But when Margaret, a petite, attractive young woman, arrived at my office for her first appointment, her problem was not fear of flying. In her soft, slightly southern accent she said, "I know you're not a physician." She smiled at the now puzzled look on my face. "I have a wonderful ob-gyn who helped me get through my last pregnancy." Four weeks into that pregnancy she had started to lose the baby. The doctor quickly put her on Terbutaline, a drug that helps prevent spontaneous miscarriage. He had raised the dosage to near maximum and had told her she would have to spend most of her pregnancy in bed.

Margaret went on. "I had to take a leave of absence from the job I love, and I had to stay in bed for the last few months of my pregnancy. It made me feel so helpless, like I was wasting my life away. My son is 3 years old. Now I'm pregnant with a girl, and I really can't stand the thought of being homebound in bed for the next few months."

I asked, "How can I help you?" I realized immediately that her case was going to be a study in conservation—preserving and protecting her baby until its birth.

She replied, "I want you to hypnotize me and instruct my body to stop the spontaneous miscarriage. I'm a good candidate." She went on to explain that during stage hypnosis she had been hypnotized, and recalled that she had laughed hysterically about an empty Coke bottle, with tears streaming down her face.

I didn't necessarily agree that just because she responded to a stage hypnotist's suggestions Margaret would be a good subject for hypnosis. However, in hypnosis, part of what we do is to have the client recall a previous hypnotic experience. If they can recall it in great detail, they will move into a hypnotic trance. Since this experience, and her overwhelming desire to carry her baby to term, were what Margaret brought to the session, it seemed reasonable to invite her into hypnosis. In preparation, we talked for a while about her life—her family, her friendships, her interests, and her job. I was looking for examples that would demonstrate that she knew how to hold onto things—for example, her high school sweetheart, who was now her husband. I also noted as we chatted that she loved to read and had hung onto treasured books from her childhood.

Then we began the hypnosis. I talked to her for a while, pacing my words with her breathing. I guided her to that empty Coke bottle that had made her laugh so hard during stage hypnosis. She started to smile and then to chuckle. She went into a hypnotic trance.

I continued with the hypnosis for 40 minutes, pointing out to her how she was a thoughtful person who tended to hold onto things that were important to her: friendships and books, to use two examples. I continued to remind her how good she was at holding onto things she cared about. I suggested to her that now she concentrate on holding onto the new baby. This meant getting in touch with the muscles that she used to keep the growing infant in utero until it was time to deliver. Before I gradually began to awaken her, I left her with the posthypnotic reminder that she imagine herself holding that Coke bottle—the funniest Coke bottle ever—between her thighs. This helped her concentrate on strengthening the muscles of her pelvic floor.

I asked Margaret to bring to the next session a pleasant memory or an object that she had had since her childhood. She came in the following week, and we repeated the hypnotic procedure. As I had requested, she brought a pleasant memory and an object. The object was a book, *The Lost Princess of Oz*. During this second session, I instructed her to spend a half hour every day with *The Lost Princess of Oz* (Baum, 1917), read a few pages, and then put the book between her thighs and gently squeeze it for a while. I also repeated periodically during these early sessions and others that followed how good she was at holding onto things. During hypnosis, I alternated between suggesting that the Coke bottle or the book, held between her thighs, were ways for her to carry her own princess to term.

A month later, her symptoms of spontaneous miscarriage had subsided. Her doctor had even reduced the amount of Terbutaline she was taking but said he would go back to the full dosage if her symptoms returned.

"They won't, will they?" Margaret asked anxiously.

"You're so good at hypnosis and holding onto things, why should they?" I responded. I felt a bit like a stage hypnotist myself for a moment, and wondered whether the performing life would be right for me. Later on, I had another opportunity to "step on the stage" with Margaret, but that's a story I will save for the concluding chapter.

The alliance Margaret and I created was based on employing the strengths she possessed when she walked in the door and incorporating them into the therapeutic process. This established our working relationship and left Margaret with more personal power and control. It was she who was controlling the pregnancy, not me or her doctor. It was also helpful for Margaret and me to review her life history. I was able to help her identify the many things in her life that she successfully held on to.

We continued our sessions for another month. By then, Margaret had become confident that she would be able to carry her baby to term, without medication and without missing more than a few days of work. In reviewing Margaret's case, I recognized my role as a conservationist. I had focused on protection and preservation. This was a role I continued to adapt with clients, and I discuss other cases in Chapter 11, "The Psychotherapist as Conservationist."

Case 2: Joe

For a trucker, there is nothing worse than being gripped by mortal fear of getting behind the wheel. Joe had been a successful over-the-road trucker, averaging $75,000 to $80,000 a year, until the accident that changed his life. One winter morning, his truck slid on glare ice into an SUV, in which there were four kids on their way to school. The SUV caught fire and the children died in the blaze. Joe couldn't get the picture out of his mind. He couldn't stand even the thought of climbing behind the wheel of another truck, but this was the only job he had ever known. He had started driving a small delivery truck when he was 19 and had driven regularly for the rest of his working life. Could I help him?

As we started to work together, Joe was guilt-ridden, anxious, and depressed. He had nightmares about the accident. He couldn't drive. In fact, he almost became physically sick to his stomach even thinking about getting behind the wheel. He was tense when riding with his wife or friends. I thought and still believe it was a clear case of posttraumatic stress disorder (PTSD). He was embarrassed at his "weakness." Joe's beer-drinking trucker buddies ridiculed him and he ridiculed himself. He realized that he needed to get past the accident and its effect on him. He said he'd never had any problems even remotely like this before.

I realized that standard psychotherapeutic approaches were not going to work with Joe, and that something was missing from his story. I began to focus on helping Joe rewrite the story of his accident.

We started cognitive behavior therapy. In this kind of treatment, therapists encourage clients to be as specific as they can in identifying the thoughts and feelings that are interfering with their lives. We generally do this by providing very specific assignments. In Joe's case, he was having trouble believing in therapy enough to do most of the assignments, but I finally found something that was familiar to him and which he agreed to try.

I asked him if his company required him to keep a log. I knew that many trucking companies do this. Yes, he said. I told him that if he started keeping a log of his thoughts and feelings he might be able to reduce his nightmares. He told me he would do "almost anything" to be able to get a decent night's sleep, even though he wasn't sure how such a journal would help.

I gave him an example: "Have you ever been in a bar and had some tough guys—maybe bikers—give you a hard time?"

"Of course!" he answered.

I continued. "Did you take them on?"

He laughed. "I'm not stupid!"

"Were you still mad at them for bothering you?"

"Of course I was!"

"So, what did you do?"

"Well, I'll tell you what I did. First I got on the radio and told all my buddies, and we all talked about what we'd do if we caught up with them."

"Then what?"

"Then I got drunk."

I suggested to him that talking to his buddies was a way of externalizing the event and that getting drunk was a way of medicating himself.

"So," I explained, "we are going to find a way for you to get this accident out of your head, and keeping a log is one of the tools we are going to use. It's just like talking to your buddies on the radio."

Joe said, "It sounds like junk, but I know how to keep a log, so I'll give it a try." I explained that he needed to bring his log in so we could review it and so I could help him modify his thoughts, beliefs, and moods. This would turn his log into a journal-log which might be helpful therapeutically. He gave me a big smirky smile. He wasn't buying much of it, but he was willing to try.

I said, "I know that you are a very independent guy. You don't like the idea of needing anybody's help. Driving a truck is your life. But if we can find a way for you to externalize some of the things you're feeling—guilt, anger, failure, fear—you may be able to get yourself out of the emotional swamp you're in." I continued, "You wouldn't drive your truck through a swamp, would you?" I barely got a smile out of him.

Six weeks later Joe was still in the swamp. The only reason he kept coming to see me, he said, was that he was still having trouble getting to sleep unless he was pretty drunk.

We kept working. After two more months, he had made a little progress. He told me, "You know, I'm starting to feel a little like my old self. If only I didn't have those terrible nightmares of fires and people screaming. I wake up yelling and dripping in sweat. Practically the only way to get back to sleep is to get drunk again."

I decided he needed medical support. It took three sessions to convince him to try medication. He went (with some reservations and another smirk) to a "real shrink," a psychiatrist I knew: I all but hand-carried him to the appointment.

The doctor put him on an antidepressant and somehow convinced him to cut back on the drinking. The nightmares started to taper off and his work with his log was allowing him some symptomatic relief. After two more months of therapy and one small increase in the medication, he was driving his car. A month later he was back driving cautiously around town in his truck.

But several sessions later, his progress seemed to be nearly at a standstill. His log showed that he still had considerable doubt and serious guilt. At my suggestion he looked at the accident report. The report, along with the interviews of three bystanders, showed that his truck had hit a large stretch of black ice on the highway and slid out of control and into the SUV. It was clear that there was nothing he could have done to avoid the accident. He got angry when he read this.

"Okay, so I wasn't to blame. Will that make the guilt and the nightmares go away?"

"Wait a minute," I answered him. "Listen to what you just said. You said—and I'll quote you just now—'I wasn't to blame.' But if you haven't made a mistake, then you are not guilty, and you don't have to feel that way."

After some months of psychotherapy and medication, the nightmares reduced in intensity and frequency. Joe was able to get back into his truck, get on the road, make a living, and start to feel like his old productive self. Once he was functioning well, his anxiety and guilt began to fade.

I was working as an "editor" with Joe, urging him to rewrite his story of the accident, a version in which he was not to blame. Asking Joe to read the accident report gave him a useful tool. It helped him deconstruct the story of his guilt. I felt that if he could understand that guilt, he could rewrite the story from a nonguilty point of view. At times, a critical remark or insight by the client will accomplish the goal that you set out to achieve. This was true for Joe, and I will discuss deconstruction as a tool for the psychotherapist as editor in more depth later in this book.

Case 3: Charlie and Suzanne

Charlie was an outstanding college athlete and Suzanne was his adoring fan. He was a great first baseman and good clutch hitter in college, and she was a pretty sorority girl and baseball fan.

When they were in college, their lives were wonderful. Then came graduation, marriage, and demanding jobs. He sold life insurance and she taught third grade. By the time they consulted me, the honeymoon was definitely over. Charlie spent many evenings with clients and the rest of the time he was out drinking with his buddies in a sports bar.

Suzanne spent most nights home alone, marking papers and preparing lesson plans. She became lonely, angry, and disillusioned. Charlie became defensive and increasingly distant. Their arguments became more demeaning and vicious. Three years into the marriage, Charlie and Suzanne saw only one solution. They both wanted out. But her dad liked having a star athlete to play golf with, and he and Suzanne's mother pleaded with them to go for counseling. So they came to see me for what they referred to as a "session or two."

One look at their flushed, angry faces told me not to ask them how they were getting along. I already knew, and I decided to avoid an immediate bloody argument by asking them my usual warm-up questions: "How did you meet?" "What did you do on your first date?" "What other fun things did you do?" "What are your plans for the future?"

Then I saw them separately and got a picture of just how bad things were.

"She's a cold, controlling bitch," Charlie said.

"He's an egotistical, demanding little boy who only wants to relive his glory days in college," Suzanne told me.

Individually they had absolutely nothing positive to say about each other. They were so pointed in their blame I decided to see if they could go back and recapture some of the joy, love, maybe even the romance they once felt.

I had discovered the exercises, checklists, and questionnaires used by John Gottman, a pioneer in couples therapy. His techniques, which he presented in workshops that I attended, had proven effective in reactivating positive feelings (Gottman & Silver, 1999).

Charlie and Suzanne had spent almost all of their married life together looking for complaints to direct contemptuously at one another. I wanted them to start seeing some of the positives. I launched what I call a "Redirection Program."

I began with an exercise called "I appreciate ...," which featured a list of some 72 mostly positive descriptive adjectives, such as considerate, affectionate, organized, and resourceful. I asked Charlie and Suzanne to select a few of these descriptions during the week and then write about an actual incident that illustrated that characteristic in their spouse. It didn't have to be current, and it required them to think back to happier times.

They both looked disgusted with the idea. I said, "If you want to save your marriage, or if you want to be able to tell your parents that you tried, then try and see what you can come up with."

They came in the following week, both still complaining bitterly about the other. She had done the assignment, drawing on incidents from 3 or 4 years before. He had done his just 20 minutes before they arrived—in the bathroom while he was shaving—and his hasty preparation showed. She told him that like a lot of things, his efforts with this task were pathetic. Her attack sparked his competitive nature. He mumbled that he would do better. I smiled at him and said, "I remember that you were always a good 'clutch hitter.'" He winked at me, acknowledging my efforts to communicate.

They went over the items she had checked and the examples she had given. This touched him, so he came up on the spot with a couple of his own about her. We had inched forward. I asked them to repeat the assignment for the following week, which they did, again with marginal success. But this time they were almost civil.

The week after that, I used Gottman's "Love Maps Questionnaire" (1999, pp. 47–60) to give them an idea of how their relationship was doing: Not so well, but better. We followed that with a 20-item true/false test of the relationship (e.g., "At the end of the day my partner is glad to see me").

We were still making progress, but not achieving any major breakthroughs. At about this time, I happened to ask Charlie what he would have done on the baseball field when a team member made a costly error. I believed that Charlie knew what to do and say under those circumstances. I thought a sports analogy might spur some thoughtfulness on his part. I also thought it might demonstrate for Charlie that I was appreciative of sports and sports ability, and would help him see parallels between playing fair on the field and playing fair in marriage.

"I'd yell encouragement and maybe go over and pat him on the back and say 'Go Heads Up. We've all booted some.'" Both Charlie and Suzanne smiled at this and I suggested that the two of them start to regard marriage as a team sport: No more criticisms; more encouragement and more affection and support. They looked doubtful, but hopeful.

After that, the marriage turned around. They came in for another 6 weeks with reports of positive loving and romantic events. At their last session they both smiled at me and said in unison, "Marriage is a team sport." This is a case where I was the psychotherapist as coach, unintentionally. I helped a couple learn how to play the sport of marriage. By adapting a sports metaphor, which was something familiar to them both, I was able to function as a coach, encouraging them to work together as a team.

These case histories demonstrate the need to adapt different roles with clients and use what they bring with them to the therapeutic relationship. For Margaret, I was able to use her ability to take care of things she loved to help her protect her unborn baby. I was able to apply Joe's familiarity with keeping a log to help him rewrite his story of a traumatic accident. And for Charlie and Suzanne, their understanding of team sports, along with my coaching, got them back on track in the game of marriage. Throughout this book, I'll describe a multitude of different roles that can be used with clients to resolve conflict, create fulfillment, and increase life's happiness.

2 The Psychotherapist as Navigator

When I contemplate the psychotherapist as a navigator, I think of a sailing ship's master in the days of sail. He was responsible for the operational navigation of the ship. The master held responsibility for everything from sails to rigging, from the helm to the ballast, from the sextant, compass, telescope, lead line, charts, and maps, from seeing that there were adequate supplies of water, hardtack, rigging, and rum to the maintenance of the log.

The psychotherapist who functions as a navigator has much to learn from these masters of the seas, who would always begin their journeys with a thorough and complete discussion with their captain about the dangers of the route. They would chart the course before leaving shore. Too often, in practice, psychotherapists, including me, do not develop a clear itinerary for their client's journey. Rather than developing a plan that would help the client conceptualize the desired outcome, I would often, early on in my career, react to the current crisis.

Consider the master of the ship who would not leave port without adequate supplies. So, too, should the psychotherapist take time at the beginning of the journey to assess the strengths, life experiences, and level of client motivation. Keep in mind that the master is responsible for laying out and maintaining an ongoing record of the ship's journey. In the same fashion, the psychotherapist is responsible for keeping accurate records of session-by-session progress through the use of measurement, testing and tracking as the client progresses on the therapeutic journey.

The psychotherapist can help the client move forward by assigning homework. The completion of homework provides the psychotherapist with yet another measurement of client motivation and progress.

Yet another parallel between the 16th century ship's navigator and the psychotherapist exists. Lead lines were used to measure the depth of the water. In the 16th century, the lead on the line had a piece of tallow attached to its surface. As the line dragged the bottom of the harbor, it collected sand, mud, or pebbles, which showed the master exactly where the ship was as it approached port once again. Likewise, knowing what's going on beneath the surface is as important to the psychotherapist as it is to the master of a ship. Biofeedback and neurobiofeedback are techniques that help the psychotherapist know what lurks below the surface of the client's mind. Later in this chapter, I describe a case in which biofeedback contributed to the therapy's success.

Mapping has other uses as well. If you have ever been lost in a strange city, you know that it can be a frightening experience. Even when you have a map, if the street signs aren't readable, you may not be able to get oriented. If you've never been in that city before, you also may not know that some sections of a town are dangerous. And if the city is in a foreign country where you don't speak the language, you desperately need a guide.

Ten years ago, my wife and I were driving in Italy on our way to a Milan family therapy workshop at a ski resort close to Verona. Somehow we had gotten off the main highway in Bolzano and needed directions. We stopped at a little restaurant. I went in and approached the crowded bar with my road map in hand and asked if anyone spoke English. At first there was an overwhelming silence, and then one woman asked in halting English, "What is the problem?"

I showed her the map and pointed to our destination. She explained to me, mostly in Italian, what I needed to do, but I didn't understand her directions. Seeing the baffled look on my face, she paused, reached for her purse, and said, "Follow me, it's not too far."

As I started my car she went past me in a blue Fiat, waved, and pumped her fist for me to speed up. She slowed as we approached intersections with lights so we could go through together. When the traffic got heavier, she slowed down, and as it got lighter, she gave me another pumped fist and speeded up. I could tell that she was monitoring my progress the whole time. We had a navigator!

You can imagine our surprise as our newfound guide drove and drove for 9 miles through narrow, twisting city streets, obviously going far out of her way, before pulling over and getting out of her car, pointing to the entrance to the highway. I offered her payment for her generous help, but she waved the offer off, gave us both a big Italian hug, and went on her way.

Before driving back onto the highway, we checked our current position on the map and realized just how very lost we had been. We then resumed our journey, now knowing exactly where we were and how much farther we had to go. As we drove, we talked about the woman's graciousness, and I realized that she had given me an excellent model for psychotherapy: the psychotherapist as navigator.

As mentioned in the introduction, my fascination with maps dates back to my days in the Air Force. More recently, I have discovered that I am not alone in applying the metaphor of the navigator to psychotherapy.

Daniel Leising, a psychologist and researcher in the Department of Psychology at the University of Halle-Wittenberg in Germany, alluded to psychotherapists as tour guides in his 2008 paper, "Applying Principles of Intercultural Communication to Personality Disorder Therapy" (Leising, 2008). In the introduction to this paper he states, "I suggest conceptualizing the situation of a patient with a personality disorder as being similar to that of an overseas traveler" (p. 261). Later in the paper, he adds, "In order [for the traveler] to successfully make [his or her way] in the strange new environment, the guest would benefit from the advice of a knowledgeable tourist guide" (p. 267).

For the psychotherapist, this may mean helping clients explore—isn't that a navigating word?—their goals for psychotherapy by determining:

Where do you want to go? What is your goal or destination?
What does the goal look like?
What is the shortest, most convenient, and safest route?
What are the strengths and capabilities that will help you get there?
What barriers stand in your way? What would prevent you from achieving your goal?
Who can help you find your way?
How can you avoid getting lost in the future?

The "journey" thus becomes a metaphor for psychotherapy, with the psychotherapist as a navigator who provides direction, helps set goals, and gives support. Leising also speaks of Pretzer's (2004) paper titled "Cognitive Therapy of Personality Disorders," where Pretzer refers to the "guided discovery" of the client by the psychotherapist (Pretzer, 2004).

Psychotherapy is generally auditory in nature. The patient does most of the talking. Yet, much learning is visual. In our daily lives, we constantly respond to visual cues without even thinking about it—traffic lights, caution signs, house numbers. For clients who are likely to respond to visual clues, the therapist can provide a course of visual action. These are often the clients who describe their experiences by beginning sentences with "I pictured," "I saw," "The photograph in my mind is...." This visual approach is a unique contribution of the psychotherapist as navigator. Most therapists would restrict themselves to the usual auditory communications of therapy.

Just as a map helps people orient to their surroundings, visual aids can be a therapist's tool for showing clients where they've been, where they currently are, and what progress they have made. In and of itself, this can be very motivating. Just as a guide points people in the direction they want to go, a therapist can help direct a client toward a goal.

For many years, therapists have used charts and graphs as a form of psychological mapping. In *I'm O.K., You're O.K.* (Harris, 1964), a simple diagram helps clients understand how they feel about themselves in relationship to others and their world. Steve de Shazer (1985), a well-known family therapist, used charts and graphs in his scaling techniques, which were built around three or four questions intended to help clients determine how they feel about themselves. Converting these responses to numbers gave clients a graph that visually depicted their emotions and attitudes. For example, the question, "Can you tell me on a scale of 1 to 5 how much better you feel about yourself?" is easily converted into a graph that tracks progress. In 1995, Michael White, in *Re-Authoring Lives: Interviews and Essays*, describes mapping techniques that allow clients to track their progress in developing a more positive sense of self. White calls this "the migration of identity," suggesting an extended journey.

Mapping techniques in psychotherapy are still in their infancy, much like the early seafarers' maps. By today's standards they are crude and limited. But as we discover the value and power of these mapping techniques, I believe the navigational approach will take firmer hold in psychotherapy.

Case 4: Bill

For this particular client, I used mapping techniques to help him shed a troublesome phobia. The map we created together helped him see where he was and where he wanted to go. It made his goal tangible and attainable. My role was to develop a therapeutic plan, plot the trip, and help Bill stay on course.

Bill was a lanky, nice-looking 17-year-old, embarrassed at even being in my office, especially accompanied by his mother, a successful professional woman. Bill's father, a decorated military officer, had died 4 years earlier.

Bill's stated problem was that he could not go out to eat. The trouble began one day when he went with some of his buddies for a hamburger and fries after school. While he was finishing his fries, he almost choked, to the great amusement of his buddies. On the way home, he started feeling sick and told the guy who was driving to stop the car. He jumped out and vomited all over the curb. Recalling that incident, Bill said, "You can't believe how all the guys laughed while I was heaving my guts out." After that, it became difficult for him to eat in public, first at fast-food restaurants, and then everywhere else, and especially if any other teenagers were present. The situation became so bad that he couldn't eat anywhere except at home.

Bill and his mother thought the problem would abate in a few weeks, but instead it became worse. Panic set in. He was in the beginning stages of a social phobia. Bill knew he couldn't take his girlfriend out for much of a date unless they at least stopped for ice cream or a soft drink, but he was afraid to do that. His social life began to falter. He had also been accepted at a couple of universities, but he was nearly frantic. "How can I go away to college if I can't go out to eat?" he asked.

After he drew this bleak picture of the problem, Bill and I got to work. There was nothing in his life history that would account for the phobia. He said his life had been going great up to this point. He had good friends, excellent grades, an attractive girlfriend, and his own car. Why, he wondered, was he being cursed with this situation now? I had no answer—except for the obvious: No one (especially a teenager) likes to be teased. His friends had teased him unmercifully. They let up once they saw how much it was upsetting him, but by then the damage had been done.

I told Bill that while I couldn't explain the cause of the problem, I could give him a treatment plan that I thought would work. Since he was on track for a career in engineering, I believed he would respond easily and quickly to biofeedback. The first thing I did was show him the EMG machine and explain how it worked. I demonstrated how the electrodes would be attached to his forehead and how the tension in his forehead muscles would actually be printed out on a graph in front of him. This was a way to get a reading of what lay beneath the surface for Bill (see Figure 2.1).

I urged him to take deep breaths and think about fun things he had done with his buddies. Then I had him look at the EMG's graph so that he could see the drop in muscle tension. The graph provided a primitive map that measured the muscular tension that his anxiety was creating.

Once we had reviewed the "anxiety map" together, we were ready to chart another map, for treatment. That map below showed us over a series of sessions how Bill could reduce his anxiety about going out to eat.

We spent the next session reviewing the impact of stress on the body, especially the digestive system. Our goal was to lower Bill's stress. I suggested he do relaxation exercises—deep breathing, imaging, muscle relaxation—four times a day and then write down in a notebook how he

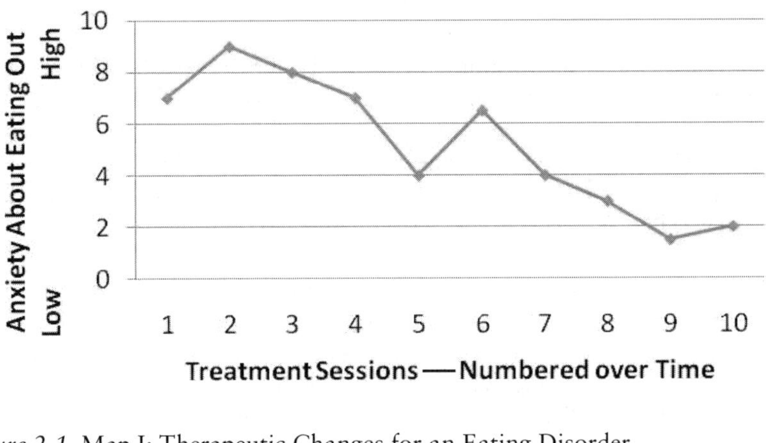

Figure 2.1 Map I: Therapeutic Changes for an Eating Disorder.

felt. During our third session, he reported success with the relaxation, but he wondered how this was going to help him with his problem.

I then introduced the idea of systematic desensitization. I explained to Bill that we would develop a hierarchy of stressful situations about going out to eat. We would start with eating at home, which we knew he could do with zero stress, and would work up to eating a hamburger and fries with his friends in a busy fast-food place (extremely high stress). As I described what I had in mind, Bill turned pale. I would have to help him feel more confident before we could proceed. I again had him watch the EMG's graphing while he practiced the relaxation exercises I had taught him. Within 12 minutes he had visible proof that relaxation could help him lower his anxiety. This made him a believer, and we were ready to get into the full treatment program of systematic desensitization with biofeedback and charting.

To begin the systematic desensitization, I got a couple of soft drinks with straws, and suggested Bill take one small sip. As he did so, I noticed a slightly surprised look on his face. When we did another biofeedback-assisted relaxation, he offered to take another sip, and was again successful. So we stopped right there and again charted his anxiety level, as shown in Figure 2.1. He could see his progress, and he told me that for the first time he felt a little hope about his condition and was anticipating leaving for college.

Before Bill left the session, I reminded him to continue practicing relaxation, and I added some eating experiences. I told him that we would be going to the park during our next session. The following week, we began with a relaxation exercise in the office, went to the park to sit on a bench and have a soft drink, and then looked in the window of a restaurant. It was very quiet, so we walked in and took a table near the restroom. Throughout the treatment, it was reassuring to Bill to know that he was just a few steps away from the toilet. He sat down and I went through the serving line and got two sodas for us. He even managed to take a sip. Wow! Major success.

The next step was adding a little food. I encouraged Bill to imagine himself eating a hamburger or fries. He chose fries, saying that they made him less queasy. We repeated the whole process: First, relaxation procedures, then eating fries and drinking a soft drink in my office, which had become a safe place for Bill, then down to the park to finish the fries. Then we tried a hamburger and soft drink, and repeated the whole process with easy success.

With these steps under our belts, so to speak, we decided to try a regular, but quiet, restaurant. Bill had no problems. At our next session we went to a fast-food place and ordered our hamburgers, fries, and soft drinks. The meal went down pretty well until a couple of high-schoolers came in. Bill dashed to the restroom. Before I needed to rescue him, he came out with a half-smile, but looking a little gray. He said he had done a few relaxing breaths to make the nausea let up, and he was all right. We left quickly anyway. I saw no reason to push our luck.

At our next session, we went to a different fast-food place, a little farther from his school and earlier in the afternoon. We started out with just a soft drink but quickly moved on to the full order (Map I, Position 5) and repeated this for the next two sessions (Map I, Position 6). Bill especially enjoyed seeing his progress on the map. Finally, we ventured back to Hardee's, where the problem had begun. Bill told me he didn't want me to be with him; he was sure he could handle it on his own. And he did. (Map I, Position 6). He reported greater discomfort, as shown on the map, but kept working on it, and by Position 7 he began to gain confidence.

After the 10 sessions shown on the map, we put Bill's therapy on an as-needed basis. While much of this case was built around biofeedback, relaxation, and systematic desensitization, the charting was an essential element. Like the navigator of a ship who assists the captain in plotting a course, I had to be careful to avoid going too far or too fast, to always stay within reach of safety (the toilet), and to make sure we charted our progress. In this instance, charting turned out to be an interesting way for Bill actually to see our therapeutic progress.

Some of my more psychodynamically oriented colleagues may wonder if Bill's phobia was a way for him to avoid leaving home, or was perhaps an indication that his mother wasn't ready for him to leave. Either or both of these motives could have been driving his phobia, but I found both mother and son well-adjusted and excited about the prospect of his attending college. I did not feel it was necessary to explore these motives and chose instead to specifically treat the phobia. This approach shortened the treatment cycle so that Bill was able to go to college in the fall. A year later his mom called me to report that he'd had a great year at college. There had been a few shaky times, but he got through them. He had earned good grades, had made friends, and was eating regularly in the cafeteria. When I saw him 6 months later, he said he had had a great first year of college.

One key principle of the psychotherapist as navigator is to see that the client gets to a home port in the quickest time possible, while avoiding dangerous waters. This makes the role of navigator a particularly valuable one if the client's problem is time-sensitive, as it was for Bill, who was leaving for school. With clear goals for therapy, a sense of time to meet those goals should be part of the equation.

Case 5: Steve and Mary

Here is another story of my use of navigational tools in psychotherapy. Steve and Mary were a sweet couple in their 30s, who had been married for 5 years. They sat close to each other on the soft leather couch in my office. Mary quickly and sadly described a wonderful marriage, filled with warmth and love. "But," she continued, "after I got pregnant, Steve's feelings about me and the marriage somehow started to cool. After the baby's birth, he became very indifferent."

Steve grudgingly said, "My feelings toward her have not changed, but she is spending all her time and her attention on Barbara Ann, our daughter. I feel like a fifth wheel." As he described his wife's relationship with their infant daughter, I sensed that he felt left out of the equation, and he seemed resentful.

I used a couples mapping technique that was still new to me then. In reading about John Gottman's work and attending marital therapy workshops at the Gottman Institute, I had found mapping to be a very simple way to measure what was happening for couples and to help me keep track of progress as I worked with them. I had been exposed to the Gottman "Areas of Change" checklist, but for Steve and Mary I felt that I needed a briefer quiz that focused on the positive aspects of the marriage.

I felt it might be helpful to identify when and how Steve and Mary had grown apart. I developed a series of questions that would measure their satisfaction at various points in their life together. The quiz I developed is shown in Figure 2.2.

Items	**Scoring**				
	+2	**+1**	**+0**	**-1**	**-2**
1. Do you enjoy each other's company?					
2. When things go wrong, do you work together to fix the problem?					
3. Do you think of your partner's happines before your own?					
4. Do you share similar values about life's issues like finances, family, sex?					
5. Do you share household tasks like laundry, gardening, cooking, childcare?					
6. Do you share common interests?					
7. Do you share religious beliefs?					

Note: +2 = very positive; +1 = somewhat positive; 0 = neutral; -1 = somewhat negative; -2 = very negative

Figure 2.2 Brief Marital Satisfaction Quiz.

I asked each of them to fill out the quiz several times. First, I asked, "Give me a picture of how satisfied you both were right after you were married." Next, I asked them to remember what they felt like soon after the birth of their daughter. Later I asked them to fill out the survey in "real time" during their therapy. Finally, we filled out the quiz when we terminated their therapy.

Then I created a map they could actually look at. That map, "Individual Life Satisfaction Before and After Birth of Child Estimated by Wife," is shown in Figure 2.3.

Using the map as an indicator, Steve and Mary could see how the birth of their daughter had decreased Steve's level of marital satisfaction alarmingly, while decreasing Mary's marital satisfaction levels only slightly. Our goal then was to bring the family together in a way that would recapture the love and warmth they had shared before the birth of their daughter.

I worked with Steve to help him understand the shift in his marital satisfaction scores from before to after the birth of their child. He knew he was unhappy, but the mapping process gave him a visual reference point. I assured him that many husbands are not prepared for the change in the level of attention they receive from their wives, and that many experience a sense of abandonment. I helped Steve understand that by becoming more involved with their daughter and sharing a caregiving role, he could help Mary reduce the exhaustion associated with being a new mother. I also talked with him about what he wanted from the marriage, which definitely included having children. This eased the sense of loss he had been feeling and helped him see his part in the growing family.

At the same time, I suggested that Mary share parenting tasks with Steve. She was reluctant, expressing concern that he could not care for their daughter as well as she could. But with my encouragement they agreed to begin sharing the caregiving. I especially urged Mary to

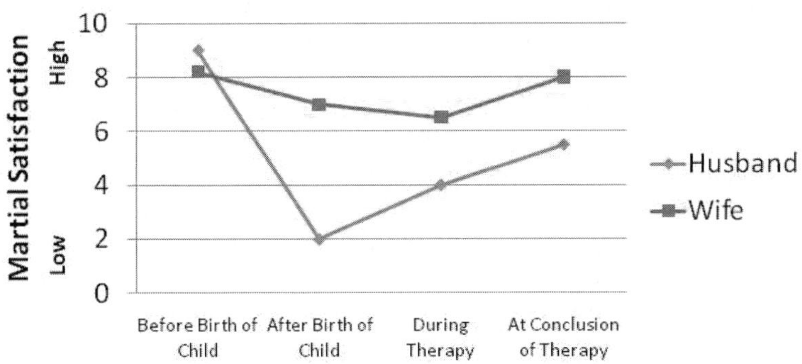

Figure 2.3 Map II: Individual Life Satisfaction Before and After Birth of Child Estimated by Wife.

include Steve in the pleasant tasks, like holding the baby after feedings. I felt that this would allow Steve to bond more closely with his daughter. At one point, he remarked with a smile that he didn't even mind changing diapers. "Baby poop really doesn't smell that bad," he admitted.

As he became a contributing father, Steve felt closer to his wife and became happier in his marriage. Reviewing the chart as we went along gave Steve and Mary visual evidence of how their relationship had expanded and made room for all three of them. They finally felt like a family. The map also told us that Steve's feeling of satisfaction had never quite increased to the prebaby level, but that he was far more positive than he had been at the beginning of therapy. Both were content with their current levels of satisfaction. It is interesting to note that as Steve became more involved in caring for Barbara Ann, Mary was less exhausted and more interested in sex. So everyone benefited.

If you were to look at the famous Lewis and Clark logs and maps of their Northwest expedition, you would note that these references not only showed the explorers where they had been, but where they could and could not go. Remember that parts of their anticipated route were blocked by snow-covered mountain peaks. Their logs and maps made it possible not only for them, but for explorers who followed them, to avoid critical mistakes and to find good paths through the mountains. For clients, as for Lewis and Clark, the mapping process not only shows where clients have been, but where they can go, and by process of elimination, where they can't or perhaps shouldn't go. This can be nicely seen in a mapping process I used when a very forthcoming, confident 50-year-old woman came to see me.

Case 6: Elizabeth

Elizabeth, who called herself Betty, was a petite woman with graying hair, bright blue-gray eyes, and a warm but hesitant smile. Her answer when I asked what had brought her to me was that she needed to find out if her husband Hank had been right for the last 32 years. He had been telling her that she was crazy for wasting her time and his money going back to school.

"When does he say these things, and why?" I asked.

"Regularly," was her reply. "He and I were high school sweethearts and we married right after we graduated. He went to work farming. He and his dad worked the big family farm together. I became a farm wife, and I have no complaints about that. We have been a successful farm family. We have three children, two boys and a girl. They are good kids, worked hard in school, got good grades, did their chores."

Betty went on to tell me that all three children went to college and that they all had good careers. The older boy studied agriculture and now worked the farm with his dad. Their daughter was a teacher, and the younger son was an accountant. She and her husband had lived a good life, Betty said. And then she fell silent.

I waited for her to continue. She had already given me a hint about the problem that brought her to see me, but if I was going to help her navigate her way to a solution I needed to know more. Finally, she spoke.

"The problem is that I have never been satisfied being just a high school graduate, and so over all the years, I've been taking classes, first at the community college and then at the university."

"When did this begin?" I asked.

"I started taking classes just after my first child was born. My husband and his dad were struggling with the farm accounts, and since I've always been good in math, I offered to help. I quickly saw that to get the accounts in order I needed some accounting background, so I took the classes in business and accounting that I felt I needed. My husband laughed and told me I was simply a farm wife and he could hire an accountant if we needed one. But 2 years and one child later, I was managing all the farm accounts and the family's, too."

Betty described how she became more and more skilled at accounting—and enrolled in more and more classes—as agribusiness grew more complex and tax laws changed. "But my husband laughed and teased me, even when the accounting firm that checked our books told him that I was doing a good job. Several years later the accountant even asked me to work for him part-time during tax season. My husband laughed about that too."

"You must have been very disappointed and angry," I commented. "It certainly seems short-sighted of your husband not to realize your value to the family business—and to him."

Betty agreed, and then went on.

"Some 20 years ago I got my degree in accounting, and he should have been proud of me. But no, it was like he was ashamed of me. After I got my degree, I started taking classes in history. I've always been something of a history buff and now I wanted to put more time into school and get a degree in history. Well, you can imagine what he says to that. He says I'm crazy, it's a waste of time and plain foolishness."

Betty assured me that she never short-changed the family or the farm. She helped the kids with their homework; her husband was always too busy with farm chores even in the winter. And it was she who encouraged the children to continue their education.

"I'm proud I did that," Betty told me. "And I'm proud of how they've turned out. So now I'm thinking of going to school full time and getting that second degree before I'm too old to care." She looked directly at me.

"So here is my question," she said. "Am I foolish or am I crazy?"

"Before I answer that question," I said, "I want you to participate in a little exercise. I'd like you help me create a map of your emotions and your life satisfaction."

She seemed puzzled but readily agreed.

First, I asked Betty to estimate her own and her husband's levels of satisfaction at various points in their lives, beginning 30 years ago when she first decided to get some further education. We then mapped that satisfaction in 5-year increments up to the present. I asked her to consider her accomplishments over the course of their marriage and also to estimate her husband's level of satisfaction at these times. The finished map, as shown below, demonstrated to Betty that for her, but not her husband, education was really a key, and as she became more educated, she increased her life satisfaction level and her self-confidence (see Figure 2.4).

I also pointed out that her husband's dissatisfaction level had not decreased as she became more educated; suggesting that at some level, despite his complaints, he had been satisfied with what she was doing.

After we reviewed the map several times, Betty acknowledged that although he had complained about her educational efforts from the beginning, he didn't really stop her. Perhaps, I suggested, he had just fallen into the habit of complaining. With a smile, I said, "The map seems to suggest that you are talking more about his dissatisfaction. You are clearly *not* crazy, and he has never been happy with your dreams and plans for education. That's what the map shows us." She agreed, smiling conspiratorially.

As I've noted, maps not only tell clients where they have been, as this map did for Betty, they can also point to places clients can't or shouldn't go. For Betty, the map became a tool of greater insight.

As we reviewed the present satisfaction ratings on the map, I asked Betty to tell me what she was seeing. She looked at the map and frowned a little. "It looks like I've been more positive and upbeat about our life together than he has. As I think about it, I've invested more in the relationship than he has, but I've always believed that is what a good wife should do."

Using the map, Betty was able to acknowledge the fact that her husband had never been quite as satisfied with life as she had, and was not

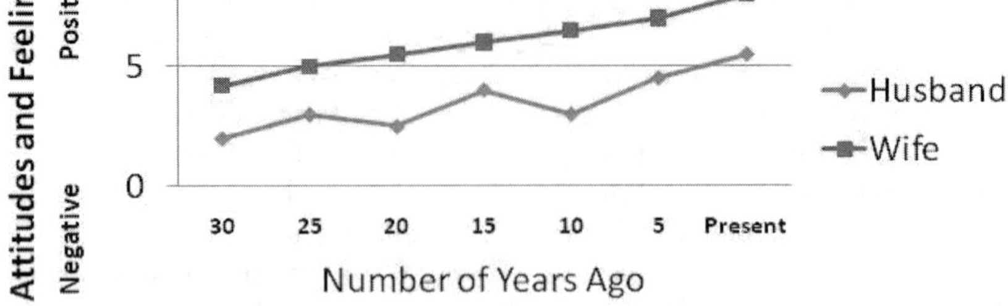

Figure 2.4 Map III: Individual Life Satisfaction for Husband and Wife, Estimated by Wife.

likely to become so. The map helped her come to grips with this and freed her up to do what made her happy. Betty also recognized that she could give herself permission to go ahead and complete her degree, which would probably increase her satisfaction more. Her accounting mind quickly grasped that, and I could see her make a decision based on her best judgment. She chose to quit worrying about what her husband said, and to do what was best for her.

She even remarked, "Well, I'm thinking I had better be thinking more about me because he won't or can't."

"And?" I asked, urging her to go on.

She smiled broadly.

"And that it's time I quit worrying about what he's thinking and really go get what I want. Go get that degree!"

At that moment I knew she would do just that. Her determination showed in her smile. When we completed the map, Betty could clearly see that she had been fulfilling her life dreams and had benefited her family and the farm in the process.

By charting her life course visually, the map validated what she had been doing. Her continuing education had made her feel better about herself, as well as giving her a sense of professional competence. She had not been wasting her time. She was not crazy. Her husband certainly didn't understand her needs or the value of her education, and as she progressed it may have made him insecure.

Betty laughed. "I've known this for years, but seeing things so graphically on the map makes it easier for me to dismiss his efforts to discourage me."

A month later, she came in for a final session with a self-commitment to spend more of her time and energy getting what she wanted, going where she wanted to go, and to stop worrying about him. She had changed. Sometimes "couples therapy" can be successful even when it involves only one of the partners.

Case 7: Paul

While most of the cases in this chapter have been examples of the therapeutic use of mapping, this particular case demonstrates what the master of the ship would call using the lead line. The lead line, as I explained earlier, is used in shallower water to determine depth. Looking below the surface, and measuring depth, is as powerful and useful a tool in psychotherapy as it is in navigation.

A handsome but somewhat tense-appearing man, Paul, came to see me because his primary physician had agreed to put him on tranquilizers, but suggested he should work on getting to the source of his tension and anxiety. Being very straightforward, I asked him to tell me what it was that had been keeping him so wired. He looked at me with as blank a look as I have ever seen, and said, "I really don't know."

When I asked him to think about what had been happening in his life that had created stress for him, he said, "Frankly, I can't think of anything."

He smiled apologetically and explained to me, "My wife and I have had our usual disagreements about money, sex, and our two boys, but that hasn't been that troubling. I make a decent living, we're buying a house we can afford, and we even save a little. Sometimes, when I look at the credit card bills, I see items that we really don't need that my wife has purchased, and that annoys me, so we go around about that. She usually explains why she bought that sweater for her mother, or whatever—and then I apologize again."

He continued, "The boys are now 12 and 14. Their clothes are a little more expensive than I would like, and the athletic shoes they wear to school cost a lot more than I think they should, so I'm annoyed about that."

"My job with the highway department can be distressing, but not much more so than anyone else's. One of my colleagues at work spends almost every Monday morning sick in bed, but that's not my problem. In other words, Doc, and this is what I told my primary care guy, I don't see any reasons why I would be getting so tense and anxious."

He went on to tell me he couldn't sleep and had little appetite. I explained to Paul that by using biofeedback techniques we might be able to measure his tension and get at the heart of his distress. At our next session, I attached the electrodes from the machine to him. This made him pretty nervous, and he broke into a sweat. After 20 minutes, he calmed down, and I began to pose some probing questions. When I asked him what he was most disappointed with currently, he explained that he was always on the verge of losing his erection. He explained, "My wife always understands and even helps me, but there's always doubt and a lot of anxiety and disappointment in my mind."

I decided to teach Paul some relaxation techniques and suggested that he try them at home. Finally identifying a problem he could actually work on, he welcomed the suggestion. I pointed out to him that after he took some relaxing breaths and did some autogenic training, the biofeedback machine reflected his relaxation and the drop in his tension. I also explained to him that he could use these techniques in bed to lower his anxiety and improve his sexual performance. He really smiled at that and was encouraged.

Next I asked Paul to look for some other major stressors in his life that we could address. He quickly identified his relationship with his father as a stressor.

"He and I have been at odds since I was a kid," Paul said. "He's a decent old man, and pretty sick right now, but he still can't resist getting on my case at every turn." I asked Paul to go back and give me more information about his father and their relationship. He told me that his father had been something of a jock and wanted Paul to be athletic too, but he was uninterested and was also too small to be good at most sports.

"I'd go out for teams," Paul said, "but was never picked, to my father's annoyance. He made me lift weights, which I hated, and was always upset when he found out I was not picked for the teams he made me try out for. And that's the way our relationship was. He would complain and I would withdraw. He's still complaining and while I get angry and upset with him, I withdraw and we repeat the same pattern."

I had Paul think about not making the team and to practice the relaxation techniques I had taught him, saying "I don't have to be on Dad's team." After a few minutes the equipment reflected his relaxation, and I suggested to him that he was getting past having to be on his Dad's team. I asked him if he knew what had happened to some of the stars of the team, and he said he didn't know and he didn't care except for Jake, who had been an outstanding athlete. And then he said, with a great smile on his face, "Jake is now a fat slob and can hardly hold a job."

I suggested to Paul that he mention Jake to his dad. He smiled and took a deep breath, and his tension level lowered considerably. He had now found a way to deal with his father's disapproval.

As I've shown, the psychotherapist who functions as a navigator is in a unique position to help clients create and then understand the maps that represent their life experiences, goals, disappointments, and satisfactions. The visual record of their therapeutic process, allows clients to see their progress. The navigator helps clients determine where they want to or need to go and helps them lay out prospective routes for getting there.

Finally, the psychotherapist as navigator encourages clients to be captains of their own fate. In each of the cases I've described, the clients themselves directed their therapy. Leising is adamant about this as well, declaring: "Rather than assuming the role of some parental authority and/or considering himself or herself a representative of the major culture, the therapist should accept the relatively modest role of a paid guide" (Leising, 2008, p. 267).

Part of my success in the case histories in this chapter can be attributed to my assumption of a modest role as guide. With guidance, Bill consistently decided what he felt he could handle. The map clearly showed Steve and Mary what was happening in their marriage after their baby was born, and it helped them take steps to reenergize their relationship. Betty's recording of her satisfaction with her accomplishments helped her realize the value of her education to herself and her family. And for Paul, obtaining visual feedback of his tension helped him identify the cause of it.

For these clients, and for others, mapping can open up a clear path of their own choosing, and send them on their way with renewed energy and confidence.

3 The Psychotherapist as Editor

In their practical guide, *Editing: Fact and Fiction*, Sharpe and Gunther (1994) describe the work of the editor in great detail. In the introduction, they state succinctly that good editing requires: "a special sensibility, a finely tuned ear, and an instinct that comes only with years of experience" (p. 1). These are skills that editors share with well-trained, empathic psychotherapists. Like editors, psychotherapists help clients review, revise, and refine their life stories. Like the writing process, the process of psychotherapy can be painful and arduous.

In my experience as a psychotherapist, one very effective way to encourage clients to review and revise their stories is to urge them to begin writing down their stories. This is sometimes called journaling, and is an alternative or sometimes an add-on to traditional talk therapy. It creates a more visual, more concrete, and more "editable" story.

Research has demonstrated the efficacy of journaling in providing another avenue of understanding for clients. Interestingly, it has also been found to have positive physical outcomes. For instance, Smyth, Stone, Hurewitz, and Kaell (1999) note in research on the effects on asthmatic and rheumatoid arthritis patients of writing about stressful experiences: "A growing amount of literature suggests that addressing patients' psychological needs produces both psychological and physical health benefits … expressive writing is one such technique that has been used successfully in several controlled studies" (p. 1289). This particular study references a brief emotional exercise developed by Pennebaker and Beal (cited by Pennebaker & Seagal, 1999) that the client writes down, commenting that "A recent meta-analysis of this written emotional expression exercise concluded that the procedure reliably improved health outcomes" (Smyth et al., 1999, p. 1289).

The work of Pennebaker, Kiecolt-Glaser, and Glaser (1988) in the *Journal of Consulting and Clinical Psychology* also demonstrates the healing power of journaling. A study they conducted, "Disclosure of Traumas and Immune Function: Health Implications for Psychotherapy," shows how psychotherapy reduced the incidence of health problems for those in the study. In the study, undergraduates who were directed to write about either traumatic experiences or superficial topics were then examined for cellular-immune system functions. The study found that confronting and writing about traumatic experiences boosted the immune systems of the experimental group (Pennebaker & Seagal, 1999).

As I interpret these studies in conjunction with my own practice, it is clear to me that journaling provides a tool for client transformation in psychotherapy. By working with clients' own writing, I have helped them recast and reconsider their life experiences in a more positive light and thus to envision a brighter future.

Case 8: Shirley

Here is one particularly memorable case in which I functioned as an editor to help a client rewrite a troubled story. Shirley was in her early 60s. At our first appointment, I asked her what had brought her in.

"I came in today because I can't sleep, I can't eat, and I can't even bring myself to go out with friends."

Thinking her symptoms sounded like depression, I asked a first diagnostic question.

"When did your life get so bad?"

"When my aunt, my mother's younger sister, died," Shirley replied softly.

"Were you especially close to her?"

"No," she answered, and started to weep.

"But you're very sad about her death now?" I was puzzled.

"No! I'm horribly ashamed." And she wept even louder.

After about 5 minutes of tears, which seemed like forever, she calmed down enough for me to speak to her again. "Maybe you could tell me what happened," I suggested.

"It started in the fall of 2004 when my mother was diagnosed with colon cancer. She told me she wasn't going to die, even after she'd had two operations. She said the same thing two years later when the cancer metastasized, and she repeated it yet again when her doctor told her that there was nothing more they could do and recommended she go into a hospice program."

But her mother refused. "That's where people go to die," she insisted. "I want to come and stay with you and your family. Then I'll have a chance."

Shirley went on to tell me that her husband and three children agreed, though begrudgingly. Her son had to give up his bedroom and move into the family room and the girls pitched in and helped a lot with their grandma.

"It worked," Shirley said, "but we were really stretched. My husband and I had to work and the kids were in school. We needed someone there during the day, but we couldn't afford a day nurse."

Shirley wiped her tears with the tissue I handed her.

"Go on," I encouraged her, wondering how the aunt entered the story.

"So, I asked my aunt, who lived about 200 miles away, if she would help," said Shirley, adding that her aunt, Catherine, was a stay-at-home mom with one 15-year-old daughter and a successful husband.

"My aunt said no," Shirley continued. "She didn't want to leave her family, even though it was her sister who was dying." Shirley and her husband struggled to care for her mother themselves, hiring day nurses and other help. It wasn't long before they went into debt.

"I asked her repeatedly to come and help," said Shirley ruefully, crying softly again, as she recalled her hurt when Catherine kept refusing and also ignoring her requests for financial help.

"Four months later, my mother died. My aunt came to the funeral and she implied to all our friends that she had helped 'all she could,' which was no help at all."

For 2 years after the funeral, Shirley and her aunt didn't speak, until Catherine developed congestive heart failure. To Shirley's surprise, Catherine called to ask for her help. She was too weak to get to the bathroom by herself, her daughter was away at college, and she was reluctant to ask for help from strangers. "My family thought I was being taken advantage of, but I went up to help," Shirley told me. And the situation was terrible. "Her husband was too busy with his business and her daughter was too busy with her friends and they treated me like I was their maid."

After 3 weeks, Shirley told her aunt she couldn't stay any longer. Catherine cried and begged, so Shirley stayed another week and then went home. Five weeks later Catherine died of a massive heart attack. Shirley went to the funeral and again was treated like a maid. She came home, at first feeling she had done her best.

"But now, 2 years later," Shirley said in a weepy voice, "I feel guilty that I neglected my aunt in her time of need." It was clear to me that Shirley had a story that was making her very unhappy. I felt that our effort together would be best spent by helping her edit her life story in a way that would provide her with a happier and more productive interpretation.

I had first developed the idea of the psychotherapist as editor when I began studying narrative therapy, which came to the forefront as a technique when it was used and promoted by Australian psychotherapist Michael White. He had been influenced by French-Algerian philosopher Jacques Derrida, and French philosopher Michel Foucault, who is best known for his studies of social institutions, including medicine and prison systems.

Both Derrida and Foucault used the term *deconstruction* in a cultural context, as part of a philosophical movement that challenged status quo assumptions about words and reality. White, who was a devotee of

Foucault's work, used the term in a more individualized way with clients, to help them challenge their beliefs and their life stories. White and Epston (1992) say, "deconstruction has to do with procedures that subvert taken-for-granted realities and practices, those so-called 'truths'" (p. 21).

In my practice, I began using the words *disassembly* and *reassembly* to describe the processes I used with clients to revise their life stories in a way that would create meaning and understanding for them. For Shirley, this meant helping her revise her story through a new understanding of her experience with her mother's, and then her aunt's, deaths. Shirley was experiencing a lot of guilt about her aunt. I wanted to help her recapture and acknowledge the anger, rejection, and bitter disappointment that she felt when Catherine consistently turned her back on the critical needs of her dying sister. Shirley was also harboring resentment toward Catherine's husband and daughter, who had treated her so shabbily.

As part of the editing process, I developed a number of questions for Shirley to consider and encouraged her to keep a journal of her thoughts. These questions were designed to escalate Shirley's inquiries into her own feelings. Some of the questions were:

- Can you make a list of all the things that your aunt and her family did for you?
- Will you rate on a scale of 1 (no guilt) to 10 (terribly guilty) how you felt when your aunt cried and begged you to stay?
- How did you feel when your aunt refused to help you?
- How did you and your family feel after your aunt pointedly ignored your requests for financial help?
- How did your mother feel when her sister refused to come to help?
- Can you compare the guilt you felt at leaving your aunt with the guilt you would have felt about not taking care of your own family if you had stayed with her?

For the next 7 weeks Shirley and I reviewed her thoughts about these questions and raised her awareness in a way that made her consider additional questions. In the 8th week of our therapy I posed a revised version of the second question: "Will you rate on a scale of 1 to 10 how much guilt you are feeling now about telling your aunt that you couldn't stay any longer?" Shirley's answer reflected significant reduction in the amount of guilt she was experiencing. I then asked her to write about all that guilt and how it was changing.

Using journaling as an editorial tool helped Shirley disperse some of her guilt. The disassembly and reassembly (revisions) of her story had helped Shirley replace her guilt with a great deal of genuine and justified anger at her aunt, and at her aunt's husband and family. Nothing about Shirley's story had been altered, but her view of the story had changed radically as we edited the story and her feelings about it. Readers might question the value of replacing guilt with anger, but I believe that guilt can be a lingering punishment, while anger, if properly directed, can be a call for action. In time, Shirley's anger became a tool that she could use to reassemble her story.

The psychotherapist as editor helps clients realize that they are the main character in their own story and helps them learn that it is within their power to determine the course of the plot, the cast of characters, and the outcome.

Case 9: Janice and Richard

The editing process can also encourage couples to edit their stories together. I usually begin with a question like, "What brings you in?" But very early in the encounter, I begin the process of editing. I ask couples questions that direct them to their own story, particularly the happy beginnings. I encourage them to talk about how they met, how they began to date, how they fell in love and decided to get married. I ask them to talk about their marriage ceremony, their honeymoon, and the early years of their marriage. Couples are relieved to move from their usually long litany of laments to the pleasurable stories.

I have adapted elements of Gottman and Silver's "Shared Meaning Questionnaire" from their book, *The Seven Principles of Making Marriage Work* (1999, pp. 246–249) in my work with couples to evoke their memories of happy times together. This helps couples break away from the adversarial climate they have created and to set the stage for what I have referred to previously as disassembly and reassembly. Gottman uses the interview as a tool to build rapport. I use it at the beginning of initial sessions to evoke the couple's memories of happy times together. This helps couples break away from the adversarial climate they have created and to set the stage for what I have referred to previously as disassembly and reassembly.

One couple I worked with, Janice and Richard, quarreled incessantly about their previous marriages and sex lives. They had each been married twice previously. These arguments dominated their behavior. Richard was particularly obsessed with hearing about her past sexual life, and had made her miserable badgering her for ever more intimate details. While it was arousing for him, it was a huge turn-off for her.

After a few sessions of private journaling, which seemed to help, I asked them to share their journal entries with each other during sessions. My intention was to help them develop greater mutual trust. As they reviewed these shared journals, it became apparent that this higher level of trust was developing. For example, some of Richard's self-doubt and feelings of sexual inferiority were reduced as Janice read his journal entries and then journaled about her own understanding and concern.

Their journaling allowed them to focus on happier times in their marriage and enabled them to replace their conflict, which had grown out of proportion, with happy memories that they could then replicate. In this way, they began to disassemble their previous story and reassemble a new one in which they both had a stake. My role, again, as an editor was helping them create a new story.

During the disassembly phase of editing, I encourage couples to challenge the story they've been living. I begin the disassembly process by taking them back to the time when they were happy: When did they first date? What were they wearing? Where did they go? What happened after the first date? Who else was in their lives at the time? When and where, and then what, up until the marriage, and then what happened? I ask them to remember when the troubles began, and encourage them to move their attention from how they *feel* about the marriage to what *happened* between them in the marriage. For example, I ask: "Who was the most affected by the behavior?" or "Who else in the family or among your friends has also been affected by the problem?" In this way, I assess the extent and the intensity of the behavior's effect on family, peers, work colleagues, social contacts, and the community.

In the editing I focus on the exceptions—the times when things did not go wrong. Then I ask the clients to explore these exceptions more fully: What happened? What did they do that gave them different outcomes than the experience that they have typically had and don't like? In many cases, the client can't envision an exception, and I work with them to imagine an exception and then to imagine how that exception would have changed their lives. For example, if a man who perceived nothing but failure were to imagine a small success, I would then ask him to go home and imagine the next morning that the success had actually happened. How would that impact his everyday life and relationships? Clients take on this exercise with the understanding that if they can make one exception they can make others. In this way, the experience becomes behavioral—external—rather than internal.

These questions create dissatisfaction with the problem, and give clients a chance to explore how the problem has affected their lives. In editing, changed attitudes and meaning can emerge. This is the editorial effect.

Case 10: Evelyn

The mind is a story-telling instrument. The editor in the psychotherapeutic setting encourages the client to tune in to successes that have always been there. This closely mirrors the tenets of the positive psychology movement. As so succinctly stated in Alan Carr's book, *Positive Psychology,* "[Positive Psychology] ... is concerned with enhancing subjective well-being and happiness" (Carr, 2000, p 1).

While many psychotherapists focus on past problems, the editing process shifts the client's attention from the past to the present and future. Consider the story of my client Evelyn, a 65-year-old woman, who had climbed a 6-foot ladder to clean her windows. As she leaned forward to reach the top window, she slipped and fell. She suffered a broken arm and a dislocated hip and was in the hospital for several days. Six months later, she was feeling anxious, having periodic nightmares, and was fearful of leaving her home. She was depressed and discouraged about her physical and emotional condition.

Evelyn was referred to me by her primary care physician because the antidepressant she had been taking didn't seem to be helping. I asked her what was troubling her the most, and she said the nightmares, so I suggested she tell me about them. She couldn't remember many details, but she said they were mostly about falling. I again incorporated journaling into my treatment, asking her to keep a "nightmare log" for a few weeks.

For the next 5 weeks, Evelyn wrote about her nightmares, in which I could see a theme of "falling, falling, falling and feeling helpless." She also began to keep a journal on the topic of how to avoid feeling helpless.

Evelyn described instances of helplessness that had been with her for years, ever since her first husband had become abusive. We discussed the marriage and the difficult divorce, and I helped her realize that she had been successful under great duress in getting out and away from an angry and dangerous man. I also congratulated her on the success of her second marriage and her significant efforts to upgrade her career. In addition to returning to school she had received a number of promotions and awards for her performance at work. As we talked, Evelyn recognized that she had worked her way out of many problems and that she had a number of successes.

Over the next month, her writing became more positive and the nightmares were all but gone. Then I suggested that she try journaling about how she would like her life to be in the future. She and her husband had always imagined a trip to Europe, but something always put the plans on hold —an emergency at her job or his, unexpected bills, or her husband's two serious illnesses. As she recounted these incidents, some of her feelings of helplessness as well as her anxiety about them returned.

With this understanding and the insight she had gained through the editing process, Evelyn began talking to her husband about her desire to take the trips they had talked about. Soon after, they began to travel. As near as I can tell, she left a significant portion of her anxiety in Dusseldorf. She did send me a smiling face postcard from Antwerp. By then we had terminated her therapy, the nightmares were gone, and she was no longer on antidepressants.

Evelyn's story is yet another example of how a new story can lead to a new sense of purpose. I had suggested that Evelyn disassemble her story in order to give up her feelings of helplessness. Editing, and the disassembly that accompanied it, helped her shift her attention to her current successful and happy life. As it did with Evelyn, this process provides clients with opportunities to see, rewrite, and re-experience the events of their lives in a more optimistic way.

Another psychotherapy process that has its roots in narrative therapy is "reframing." Sometimes the therapist discovers that clients do not need a total rewrite, but rather a shift in the way that they view their lives. When people make judgments about themselves, they usually begin with their most basic view of their current situation and themselves. Often, this view becomes a cognitive or emotional anchor. As Daniel Kahneman explains in his best-seller, *Thinking, Fast and Slow* (2011), this self-view can be modified, but it can only shift a very short distance from the anchor. Changing the anchor's position through reframing can help clients start at a better place where they possess greater control and greater opportunities for change. Kahneman explains that helping reframe people's questions can help them move their anchors a considerable distance.

Let's take the example of a young man who has a grade point average of 2.85, when a 3.0 is needed to graduate. To work with this student, the psychotherapist may begin by encouraging him to raise his grade point substantially. The 3.0 grade average represents an anchor to the student and also an insurmountable challenge. That anchor creates feelings of helplessness and defeat before he has even begun.

But where is the rule that says we must tackle the whole messy problem at once? Instead, the psychotherapist moves the anchor and creates a goal that seems actually attainable and that will present the student with the very real possibility of success. A good starting point might be one course where the student is doing fairly well. With slight extra effort, he might raise his grade from a C to a B.

This reframing requires the student only to raise his grades in a single course, a goal that he can easily envision. "But wait!" as TV ads say, "There's more! You don't have to drop the anchor there!" This student is most likely academically indifferent. So perhaps the anchor should be changed to a challenge not to skip classes and to attend class with all assignments done—no expectation of grades here, just of behavior. This also presents a measurable anchor or goal. In a near-perfect example of reframing, the psychotherapist as editor has created achievable goals for the student.

Kahneman points out that another reframing might be to ask the student to think about students he knows who have raised their grade point average, and to talk to them in order to find out how they managed to do it. This gives the student an active assignment. Again, it is measurable, specific, and helps the student find a reward system at least weekly for this new, more productive academic performance.

What he calls "broad framing" is another example of Kahneman's thinking that has application for psychotherapy. He provides an example from the performance of the stock market in the past few years. He observes that many investors and many funds managers panicked at the sudden drop in the Dow because of what he calls "loss aversion." Kahneman, who received the Nobel Prize in economics, suggests that investors "broaden the frame" by not reacting to daily shifts in the stock market. Instead, they should watch trends over a period of time, maybe quarterly. This kind of broad reframing also applies to many challenges in psychotherapy.

Imagine a client in a psychotherapist's office reliving the argument she had the previous night with her partner. Broad framing can allow her to review the last 6 months of the relationship instead of last night's horrible fight.

A few more examples of reframing can be found in Chapter 5, "The Psychotherapist as Artist." In that chapter, I show how the focus and coloring of a client's experiences can actually be visually reframed.

Another process that the psychotherapist as editor uses is clarification, which changes the language clients use when they talk and think about themselves and their lives. I encouraged Shirley to change the theme of her story from "always guilty" to "a caring person (who sometimes felt guilt)." And in persuading Evelyn to give up her "helplessness" and focus on her "successes" I was acting as an editor. I activated the healing process by changing her language. These changes can be fairly subtle. When "I am helpless," is changed to "I feel helpless at times," it represents a major shift in clarification.

Case 11: Patricia

My client Patricia was widowed when she was 50, and came to me for therapy 18 months later. She got right to the point.

"Dr. Miller, I've come in because nothing is going well for me right now."

She stopped there and seemed unable to elaborate. I asked her to tell me when things had started going bad.

"My husband died a little more than a year ago. But things got bad before that, maybe 2½ years ago, when he started getting really sick. Up until then, even though he had heart problems for years, we had had a good life. But as his health failed and he could do less and less, I realized how dependent I had become on him. We both had decent jobs, so money wasn't a problem. He was an excellent golfer, so we did a little of that. I wasn't very good. I had never been much of a cook, so he did almost all the grocery shopping and all the cooking. My job was to keep the house clean and neat, which I enjoyed. As he became weaker, I took over the cooking and while he didn't complain, I know he was never happy with meals I provided."

Patricia looked down and twisted a tissue in her hand. In addition to her inability to please her husband with the food she served, she told me, during this time the yard had gone to ruin. "A disgrace to the neighborhood," her husband said toward the end of his life.

"Both he and his garden died," Patricia declared mournfully.

"That must have been a terrible time for you," I sympathized.

It had been a very lonely time for Patricia. They had no children. There were no relatives on her side of the family and only two distant cousins on his. He had some friends on his job and she had a few at hers but nobody really close.

"Frankly, we had been so intimate that we just did things together; there didn't seem to be a need for other friends," she admitted. "So when he died, I found myself desperately alone. I've been trying to get some friendships going, but I'm afraid I've been kind of clinging, so people have shied away, and I don't blame them."

Patricia went on. "Now my job is going to hell, too. About 2 months ago we reorganized and I got a new boss, who I swear, wants to get rid of me. She never has a good word for me and 2 weeks ago she gave me a warning because I had turned off my computer 5 minutes before quitting time, which lots of people do. I went to my union steward to complain about it." Patricia added that she always arrived at work early, almost never took time off, and that her evaluations had been excellent up to then.

"I'm a good worker," Patricia said. "So I went to the steward and now my supervisor is furious at me for that. I can't seem to do anything right." And with this she burst into tears.

It would have been easy to begin therapy with Patricia that would help her "fix" the wrong things she was doing. But this was a hard-working, conscientious woman who I was sure was doing a lot of things right. My job was to help her identify the positive things she was doing.

Like Evelyn, Patricia did not need a radical change in her life story, but rather, a shift in the way she viewed it and the words she used to describe it. I began by asking her about her job situation, because this seemed to be an area where she had had some real successes, despite her frustrations. She had proven herself competent at work, while, as an introvert, she had never been that confident about her social skills.

I said to her, "It sounds like you were brave and stood up for yourself when you went to the union steward. Sometimes they are so busy at their own jobs they don't follow up as quickly as they should. Could you go back and check with the steward, pointing out that things are getting worse rather than better?"

"You mean without making it any worse?" she asked, almost half smiling.

"Maybe," I replied. "It can't get much worse," I added, almost half smiling back.

We had a task Patricia could do without too much risk—I hoped. She marched out of the office with her head a little higher. I detected a sense of hope in her.

At our session the following week Patricia told me that her second meeting with the steward went okay. "She wasn't as helpful as I needed, so I told her so." This is an example of Kahneman's concept of shifting the anchor: Patricia shifted her anchor from her own performance to her interaction with the steward, and she was able to ask for what she wanted. Patricia continued, "She suggested that if I wasn't happy I should ask for a job transfer. She even said she would help make that happen. I went home that night and wrote in my journal that I had pushed ahead. I was getting the feeling that I wasn't as helpless as I had been feeling."

Editing Patricia's story and shifting her attention away from her loneliness and frustration allowed her to take back control of her life and feel some modest success. In preparation for our next session, I reached into my file and took out a diploma. I completed the form, filling in Patricia's name, the date, and a notation that as of this date she had graduated from the School of Helplessness and Hopelessness. After the next session, in which she continued to show a take-charge attitude, I presented the diploma to her with a few typical graduation remarks, including my belief that she would continue to take charge of her life. She left the session clutching the certificate and smiling broadly. Graduation is a ritual of completion, which is a technique used by David Epston and Michael White (1990) in narrative therapy.

The job transfer didn't happen as quickly as Patricia had hoped. When her supervisor got word of it, things at work got a little worse. But Patricia was determined, and she talked to the steward again about the job transfer. Her persistence paid off. She learned that the people in the section she was slotted to be moved to had checked her work record and they were looking forward to having her join them.

After Patricia's first day on the new job, she reported that even though she was very nervous and worried that they might not like her, she found that the new job was enough like the old one that she was able to hit the ground running. Her new supervisor and her coworkers welcomed her. It was gratifying for Patricia to see that she was making progress, and it motivated her to make positive changes in other areas of her life.

The next thing Patricia wanted to tackle was her loneliness. I asked her why, since she was basically a warm and friendly person, she didn't have a wide circle of friends. My question sparked her curiosity. She promised to think about that.

The following week Patricia happily told me that she was continuing to succeed on the job and was feeling confident. She had also thought about my question and realized with some anger that, as she said, "It was partly my husband's fault. He had such a full social life at work that he preferred quiet evenings at home to going out with friends. We did very little socializing together. My friends drifted away after I got married and I let it happen."

"So what are you going to do about it?" I asked. The disassembly and reassembly process began again for Patricia.

"I've already started. I've been on the Internet contacting old friends and most of them are understanding and welcome me back. How about that?" she remarked happily. One of her lost friends suggested getting together for dinner, "Like we used to do in the old days, and we had a great time catching up! It was almost like there had not been some years' gap in our friendship." Another old friend told her that she had always felt bad when they drifted apart, because Patricia had never had time for her any more. So they both enjoyed making up for lost time.

I asked her to continue to reach out to lost friends, and also to use her revitalized social skills to make new ones. Several weeks later I asked her whether she was ready to graduate from the "School of Loneliness." "No," she answered and smiled slightly, "but I'm working on it and it feels okay." A few weeks later, after she reported enjoying a weekend with friends, we had another graduation ceremony with a "Permission to Have More Friends" diploma.

This completed the editing I did with Patricia. Two years later she sent me a note, checking to see if I was still in practice in case she needed to see me. I replied I was still on duty, as any good editor would be.

I have shown in this chapter how the psychotherapist, functioning as an editor, helps clients to review, disassemble, and eventually reassemble their life stories. This reframing, and the clarification that accompanies it, helps clients take ownership and authorship of their life stories. It is the job of the therapist to help clients recognize that it is within their power to acknowledge the plot, characters, and outcomes of their stories. In *Editing: Fact and Fiction* (1994), Sharpe and Gunther reflect upon the relationship editors have with their authors: "At different times they feel protective, supportive, affectionate, responsible, impatient, exasperated and/or frustrated, but without exception they care" (p. 140). It is these qualities that make the editing process so effective and so illuminating for both therapist and client.

4 The Psychotherapist as Banker

In banking, accuracy and attention to detail are essential. Most banking customers insist that their financial information be confidential, so bankers must be discreet. They usually possess courtesy, tact, patience, and good communication skills. They are able to help customers solve problems and keep their assets organized.

The psychotherapist as banker performs a similar role with clients. In psychotherapy, transactional analysis is the method that most closely mirrors the activities of a banker. When the psychiatrist Eric Berne, developed transactional analysis in the 1960s, he observed that in interactions between individuals, people were often communicating their feelings as well as information.

Berne explained this theory in his bestselling 1964 book, *Games People Play*. Berne described "games" that people engage in to get the better of one another. Consider the blame game. Imagine that Harry bumps into Larry at a cocktail party and spills his drink on Larry's new tie. Harry says to Larry, "Look what you made me do!" transferring the blame from the spiller to the innocent bystander. The spill then becomes Larry's "fault."

Another game is called "Yes-But." A wife says, "Why don't you change those socks? Black would look better than brown." "Yes," the husband replies, "but these are more comfortable." The wife, trying to accommodate, offers to look for other socks in his drawer. "Yes," says the husband, "but we don't have time. We'll be late." "It'll only take a minute," the wife says. "Yes," answers the husband, "but that's too much trouble." Only one person can win the yes-but transaction, and in this case it's the husband.

Berne became aware that almost all transactions between people are cumulative, and have either positive or negative effects, in much the same way that banking transactions either add to or take away from an account balance. In human interactions, as Berne saw it, the transactions are emotional rather than financial. Positive emotions make us feel good. Negative emotions make us feel bad. Some emotions, positive and negative, remain in our emotional bank accounts for a long time—perhaps many years. These accounts become a snapshot of what we are worth. That picture in turn impacts our self-esteem.

How do interpersonal interactions wind up in our emotional bank accounts? A friend becomes increasingly neglectful; she doesn't return your phone calls; she is late for a lunch date, talks the whole time on the phone, and leaves abruptly. Telling your friend that you are angry would be a healthy response, but might elicit anger in return. Instead, you might keep your feelings of anger or rejection to yourself. The cumulative effect of such experiences goes into your affect, or feelings account.

You might test such a relationship, putting pressure on the friend. Unwittingly, you might ask for proof of that person's friendship, and friendships that end are caused by exactly this kind of dynamic. People are usually unaware that they are sending such hurtful messages. Even when we confront them, they may accuse us of being "oversensitive." The behavior remains the same, and that has a dragging effect on the relationship—another drain on the emotional bank account.

Research has shown that cumulative feelings of hurt and rejection lead to social isolation. Significantly, too, it's been found that such feelings can actually suppress the human immune system. One ground-breaking cited frequently found that individuals lacking social and community ties were more likely to die within 9 years than those who had more extensive contacts (Berkman & Syme, 1979). Since this study was published, the relationship between the immune system and social isolation has been further investigated. One such study related lower levels of social ties to higher incidents of the common cold.

The psychotherapist functioning as an emotional banker can help clients become more aware of the value of emotional transactions. He or she can encourage clients to keep positive emotional balances and build their accounts for the future.

Another hallmark of Berne's work is the concept of "stroking." We may think of a "stroke" as a medical emergency but Berne used the term *stroking* to describe the effects of human interaction. He explained that stroking could be used as a fundamental unit of social action (Berne, 1964). Berne was also one of the first to recognize that any social interaction at all had a biological advantage over limited or no interaction. He was well aware of Levine's experiments with rats, which demonstrated how intensive contact affected the biochemistry of the brain and even resistance to leukemia (Levine, 1960).

Recognition is a synonym for the word *stroke* when used in this context. Recognition can be an action: a word, a look, a touch, or some other signal, spoken or unspoken that recognizes the other individual. When such recognitions are exchanged, they become a type of emotional currency.

After Berne coined the word *stroking*, psychologist Jim McKenna developed a Stroking Profile, which was first published in 1974 in the

	Stroke Interactions with Others				Personal Use of Strokes						
Stroke Value											
+4											
+3											
+2											
+1											
	Give	Refuse to give	Ask for	Reluctance to ask	Own	Reject	Mark down	Mark up	Self - stroke	Modify	Re - activate
-1											
-2											
-3											
-4											

Figure 4.1 Stroke Economy Chart.

Transactional Analysis Journal. McKenna's strokes included "giving," "taking," "asking for," and "refusing to give." I modified McKenna's profile, developing a Stroke Economy Chart to use with clients and as a teaching tool in my classes. The categories I used on this chart are: "give"; "refuse to give"; "ask for": "reluctance to ask"; "own"; "reject"; "mark down"; "mark up"; "self-stroke"; "modify"; and "reactivate" (Miller, 1976). This chart measures emotional deposits and withdrawals in interactions with others and appears in Figure 4.1.

When I use the chart with clients, here is how I explain it: "A Stroke Economy can be maintained much like a bank account. Every time you experience a major deposit or withdrawal, make a note of it. Keep track of what is happening to the economy. Note the change on the chart." I often use the analogy of balancing a checkbook. I suggest to the client that they make note of the major strokes they received or gave that week. By noting which of the categories in this chart they have used in their own emotional transactions, clients become more aware of what is available to them in their own emotional accounts.

Case 12: George

George, a World War II veteran in his late 80s, lived in a nursing home and felt lonely and neglected. He had been wounded in combat and had been disabled for a long time. He was alert and capable of carrying on a conversation. He knew where he was and loved mealtimes. He also loved repeating the story of how he won the Silver Star; he told it so often that the residents at the nursing home would walk away from him when he started telling it. This rejection never stopped him from telling the story. He received very few emotional strokes as he repeated the story, yet, with no recognition, he had very little currency in his emotional bank.

On one of my visits to him, I said, "You were a real hero in that battle. I'd be interested in learning what happened to you as you were growing up to prepare you for such an act of courage."

George told me all about how he had been a football hero in high school. It was an interesting story, and I told him so. This brief recognition motivated George to interact in more varied and appropriate ways with the other residents and with visitors. He talked about football, his job after he left the service, and his relationship with his late wife. He was now gaining positive strokes from other chapters of his life story, and was exchanging them now for more positive strokes in the present. George's experience demonstrates how even a small change and reactivating strokes can have a huge impact.

Studies of severely depressed nursing home patients have shown the positive impact of activities like bingo. Even though some residents participated unwillingly, they began to cheer up when they started playing. The gain was not the bingo prizes but the interaction itself. These patients were able to put strokes in their emotional accounts, and had them to give to others (Logsdon & Teri 1997, pp 40-45).

Individuals' stroke economies are driven in part by what they do for a living. It has been my experience that men are particularly likely to identify their worth with their work. When they are downsized, fired, quit, or retire, they lose not only economic income but emotional and social income as well.

Case 13: Roger

Roger, a 44-year-old information technology whiz, lost his job during the 2008 economic downturn. Both his income and his social interactions were connected to his business. He had few hobbies or friends outside of work. He became severely depressed. He was literally closing his emotional bank account. Because he didn't know who he was without his career, he withdrew from social situations. The fewer interactions he had with others, the fewer strokes he received. His emotional account was depleted. With my encouragement, he began to volunteer at a Speakers' Bureau and began recovering his self-esteem. He had an answer to the question, "What do you do?" As he identified with his new volunteer work, his stroke economy improved. Six months later he got a job very similar to his old one, but continued to pursue other interests and to work with the Speaker's Bureau. His depression lifted, and we were able to close his case, having done an intervention to help him from completely emptying his emotional account.

Case 14: Leland

Leland, a 34-year-old computer technician, came to see me after his wife divorced him. He was feeling desperately lonely. His father had abandoned the family when Leland was 7. He had a working mom and two younger sisters. Quiet and shy, Leland had had few friends as a child and no close friends in high school. After high school he went to a technical institute because he had always been interested in computers. The other kids called him a "computer nerd," and he defined himself that way. After graduation, he went to work for a small computer firm, installing, repairing, and updating the equipment. He married a friend of his sister's and throughout his marriage, his wife was closer to his sister than to him. He never had anything to say to her, and she wasn't interested in computers. After 3 years she asked for a divorce, saying that he never talked to her, which he admitted was true. Now he felt abandoned.

A review of Leland's stroke economy revealed that he had a limited emotional portfolio. He did not know how to give or receive positive strokes. Leland was socially isolated. He is not alone in this. A 2006 study funded through the National Science Foundation and conducted with the assistance of Lynn Smith-Lovin, a Duke University sociologist, indicated that "Americans are far more socially isolated today than they were two decades ago" (Vedantam) After I helped Leland understand the ideas behind a stroke economy, I encouraged him to give the most modest of strokes to someone else. I suggested that he say good morning to the security guard in his building. I also asked him to develop an e-mail stroke economy, since he was actually more comfortable exchanging strokes electronically than in person. He e-mailed colleagues and a few friends on a regular basis. These were introductory ways to reduce his isolation through the use of the stroke economy.

I asked him to keep a log of when he said something in passing on his way in and out of the office. I encouraged him to go out of his way to speak to some of the people he regularly encountered—the teller at the bank, the check-out person at the grocery store. Because personal interactions made him uncomfortable, he had even made a habit of going to a different barber shop every month. I suggested that he go regularly to a small, friendly neighborhood barber shop, so that he could build some casual relationships. He enjoyed gardening, so I suggested he go to the landscape center and talk to some of the regular clerks there.

Once Leland became more comfortable with these simple activities, we took a small step forward. Instead of just saying hello, for instance, he practiced asking open-ended questions of the teller and the grocery store clerk—"Are you having a good day?" or "Are you going to watch the game later?" or even "What do you think of this weather?" opening up the opportunity for an exchange. I also encouraged him to remember how people responded to his questions. If they talked about their child being out of school sick, or their new cat, he was to ask them about it next time he saw them.

This sounds like basic social skills training, and it's important to note that Leland clearly had not had this training as a kid. With guidance and encouragement from me, plus the feedback of positive strokes from others, over a 6-month period he developed a limited stroke economy. For him, a limited stroke economy was a good start.

After a few months Leland had gone out to lunch with a coworker and attended a movie with some people he met at the gym. He was even dating a bit. He was satisfied with himself and his economy at that time, so we ended our sessions. His experience suggests that the psychotherapist as banker must sometimes teach clients the very basics of a stroke economy.

Let's take a closer look at some of the other basic operations of the stroke economy. The story of Leland illustrates the first way people manage their stroke economies: by "giving." We give many kinds of recognition, positive and negative, to other people. When we reach out, even just nodding at someone when we pass by, we are recognizing their existence. We give and receive many of these strokes in a day; most hardly register and few are remembered or recalled. Something has to distinguish a stroke as out of the ordinary for it to stay in the memory account.

Here's an example of that kind of memorable stroke. Every day on her way to a coffee break, my secretary would pass a mailman. She would smile at him and say "Hi," and every day for months he would do the same. One day he didn't respond. She registered that event in her economy with puzzled feelings. The next day the same thing happened, and on the third day it happened again. On day 4 she didn't say anything to him. After that she pretended not to see him. She had, in effect, closed the account with the mailman.

About 6 weeks later, he said "Hi," as she passed him. For the next week, he regularly spoke and she responded. At the end of the week, she stopped him and asked how things had been going for the last several months. He seemed surprised, but explained that his mother-in-law was gravely ill. His wife had been staying with her, and his children were upset. This information strengthened this casual relationship and they now shared even more significant strokes: "Hi, how's your family?" "Fine, how about yours?" The story of the secretary and the mailman demonstrates how an account can be opened and closed—and opened again.

"Owning" strokes is accepting a stroke from someone else. At this point it's natural to place a value on it. Is it worth $1? $5? More? You put it into your account with the giver's name on it. If a colleague praises your work, and you agree with her assessment, the stroke has significant value—say, $10 or $20. If your firm's general manager comments on that comment, the value can go up to $50 or $100.

These values are highly personal. For instance, if you leave the house with an empty emotional portfolio, a "hello" and a smile from the mailman may be valuable. However, if you've just gotten off Skype with four people in your family who were making demands on you, you might brush right past the mailman.

Under most conditions, negative strokes are more significant to us and are more likely to be put in our emotional accounts. To understand why, imagine that you are going through your monthly credit card bill. You see a number of purchases that gave you pleasure—a fine dinner, a good book, a new pair of shoes. But if you bought a piece of china that arrived cracked, you will remember it forever. Likewise, all the month's accumulated "good mornings" do not have the weight of one "You SOB!" as you are being jostled in line. Negative strokes create emotional and physical hurt. The experience of a sick headache or upset stomach after a particularly virulent encounter with someone is common.

I have been astonished in my years of practice by young parents who tell me they are crushed because their 4-year-old screamed, "I hate you!" after they set reasonable limits—limiting Halloween candy, for instance. That negative stroke, inflicted by the child they love, has made more of an impression than the 10 or 15 positive strokes—smiles, hugs, or conversations—the parents might have gotten from their children that day. The psychotherapist functioning as a banker can help parents minimize the value of the negative strokes they receive from their children through the use of positive strokes.

Consider another example of a negative stroke that keeps impacting for a lifetime. One of my clients related an experience from second grade. On her first day in second grade, a child overhears her teacher refer to her as "chubby." For a second-grader, this is a significant negative stroke. She carries it with her into her middle-school years, when she becomes afraid of being fat, and spends years dieting. Many years later, one former chubby girl who had experienced this told me, "No matter how nice I am told I look, the compliments make no difference; I still see myself as the chubby girl."

Each day, many of us are literally swimming in a stroke environment. We know that teenagers' text messaging has vastly increased the amount of strokes being generated and transmitted. The risk of receiving hurtful and damaging strokes may well be going up significantly, thanks in part to the high use by preteens and teenagers of the Internet and cell phones. As a therapist, I function as a banker with clients in the therapeutic environment to help them interpret and manage the strokes they receive. In addition to advising and counseling clients, I also serve as a mentor, teaching clients, particularly teenagers and young adults, how to recognize and avoid negative strokes, such as those that are perceived as bullying.

It is important to recognize that negative strokes can be beneficial as well as harmful. Negative strokes, if used correctly, can help clients improve their performance or correct inappropriate behavior. Negative strokes establish limits for human behavior. Children who are rarely told "no" can become tyrants. In fact, some negative strokes can actually be instructive. Consider the man whose colleague says, "You're not really going to wear those scuffed shoes to work, are you?" Since they both know that their boss is judgmental about appearance, the colleague may be trying to help his friend. But this comment is still a question that imparts a negative stroke.

Negative strokes can be helpful if we can get past the emotional loading that goes with them. By emotional loading, I mean the offense that people take when comments are made about their appearance, language, or thinking. For example, the woman who has spent several years in West Texas can become self-conscious when even her closest friends smile at her "cowgirl" accent. Even well-meaning friends will say, after she has made a comment, that she "just got here on horseback day before yesterday." That hurts her, but she needs to understand that if she wants to fit in she needs to be careful about the West Texas slang she uses. Her friends may be trying to be helpful and help her fit in, or they may be trying to be hurtful. It's important to distinguish one from the other.

People often refuse life lessons that would make things better for them in order to avoid emotional pain. Because the banking role in psychotherapy relies largely on encouraging clients to notice emotional transactions and learn from them, I am able to help clients identify useful information and discard the emotional baggage that accompanies it, rather like the way one keeps the bills that come in the mail but throws out the inserts that come with them.

Given the emotional nature of most negative strokes, it's no wonder that many people aren't comfortable giving them. They have been taught never to say a discouraging word. Sometimes, when people don't give appropriate negative strokes, they can add them to their own account, accumulating more and more negative complaints and grievances until they sometimes feel overwhelmed and explode. Holding onto a stockpile of negative strokes creates feelings that are difficult or even impossible to process.

Case 15: John and Mary

The concept of negative strokes was a central feature in my treatment of John and Mary. John was fundamentally quiet and passive. Yet Mary told me she never knew when his temper would explode if she did something that annoyed him. She said that she was truly frightened of him. For his part, John explained that he had learned to avoid conflict. "In my family, no one dared say anything to Dad because he had a terrible temper. He never could control it, and to some extent, I can't either. It's genetic."

After explaining the concept of negative strokes to both of them, I asked Mary to try to become more aware of the small things that she was doing that annoyed her husband. For example, John had mentioned that when they were leaving home to go somewhere together, Mary would return to the bathroom three times to check her makeup. When they had friends in, she hovered over them, overfilling their drink glasses. A big annoyance for him was when she would interrupt and correct his stories, saying "No, that didn't happen in Nashville, that was Orlando." I suggested that Mary refrain from some of these "negatives."

Mary was surprised that the therapy required her to do some changing. I also asked John to share these smaller annoyances with Mary—in other words, to provide negative strokes. At the next appointment, they told me that to their surprise his temper had improved. Perhaps, I suggested, the temper wasn't genetic after all and could be controlled by airing grievances rather than storing them in his emotional portfolio.

Case 16: Jamie

Sometimes negative strokes need to be understood and modified to the client's advantage. A client named Jamie told me with genuine sadness that in his hurry to get ready one morning he had worn a bizarre and inappropriate tie to work. Two of his coworkers pointed it out to him. One of them said, "Sometimes you dress like a hick." Ridiculing his tie was a little like a negative stroke, which he may have been able to dismiss. But when it was inflated into an observation about who he was, "a hick," it took on significant power. Strokes like this can be major deposits into an individual's emotional account and affect self-image.

After Jamie and I talked about this incident, he became more selective about his ties and his appearance in general. At one point, he was able to look at himself and say, "I'm not a hick!" In fact, he is now waiting for the day when someone will say, "You always look so nice." At that point, the "hick" remark is paid in full, canceled out.

Clients such as the ones I've described can benefit from learning why they carry such large balances of negative strokes. For Jamie, I suggested that the offending coworker had his own negative strokes. I asked him, "How important is this guy's opinion to you?" These are the kind of questions we should all ask ourselves before depositing negative strokes into our emotional accounts.

Clients benefit from the tools the psychotherapist can give them to challenge the validity of negative strokes. For a stroke economy to work well, clients have to develop a stroke filter, which will allow the nurturing, sustaining part of a stroke to pass through while setting aside the negative emotions that come with the stroke.

Another step in the stroke evaluation process I undertake with clients is to challenge them to translate the messages they are receiving in a different way, and take into consideration the other's perspective. For instance, suppose an elderly aunt has said to a client, "I feel that you really don't like me since you only see me once a month." Under examination with the client, this is usually more about the aunt's neediness than about the client's inadequacy as a niece or nephew. The psychotherapist can work with the client to add up the positive impacts of the relationship with the aunt, while filtering out the hurt and guilt that the aunt inflicts. Such examination helps clients understand that they have some control over their own emotional account.

Another important thing the psychotherapist does in the banker role is help clients learn how to ask for the strokes they need or want. There is real skill in doing this the right way, at the right time, and with the right intensity. Becoming too demanding, clients may generate resentment or a negative stroke in return instead of the positive stroke they requested. Often clients see me because their stroke accounts are depleted. They have developed habits and activities that do not provide a return on their emotional investments.

For instance, a client who is spending an hour a week with someone really hateful might explore that behavior with me. Helping the client understand what such a relationship is doing to their stroke economy might encourage that client to be more selective about his relationships.

Another thing that I help clients realize is that asking for strokes may backfire. This is one of the reasons why people don't try to generate more strokes. They may feel that they do not deserve them, or fear rejection. As a banker in my psychotherapy practice, I help clients measure the real value of negative strokes. This helps them assure that their emotional portfolios are operating, as bankers say, "in the black."

People can also ask for negative strokes by acting stupid, annoying, or mean. When others request negative strokes from clients, it's important to help them discover that they have choices. Clients learn that they can refuse to give others strokes, give others the strokes they requested, or give them other strokes than those they requested. One simple example of refusing to give is the reaction one might have to the unsolicited fund-raising call. We can fairly easily say no, or "refuse to give" in such a situation. With friends and families, however, it gets more difficult.

Here's a personal example of how hard it can be to "refuse to give." One of my wayward uncles called me and said, "I've just gotten out of the hospital and I'm nearly broke. Will you send me $50?" So I did. A few months later he called a second time, telling me he was hungry, asking for $50 again. I sent it. The third time, he called with the obvious noise of a bar in the background. He asked for another $50. In the meantime, I had learned that he had been in an alcohol rehab program twice in the past year. I finally realized that I was an enabler. That allowed me to say a friendly no, or to refuse to give, in transactional analysis terms.

My experience with clients has led me to identify a characteristic in the stroke economy that I call "reluctance to ask." Often, people are embarrassed to ask for anything. Imagine that you have put extra time and effort into a project at work. It wouldn't be wrong for you to let management know about your dedication and effort. But many of us would be reluctant to say anything like that, knowing that if our efforts are not acknowledged, we'll be disappointed.

When the request is more emotional, it can be even harder to ask. There can be a quality of near-desperation in asking a partner for a special acknowledgment of his or her feelings for you. It puts you at risk, because if the partner refuses, it will make you more vulnerable. That causes us to hold back. A good psychotherapist has a responsibility to train his or her clients to ask for what they need and want.

Another component of a stroke economy is rejecting a stroke. Parents teach their children this when they warn them, "Don't accept candy from a stranger." As a psychotherapist, I can help clients assess the value of strokes, and to reject those they don't want or need. Many fairy tales teach us that not everything offered is good for us. The classic example is Snow White, who was offered, and took, the poisoned apple. Clients who have lived under the false belief that they must accept almost anything offered are often suffering from a depleted stroke economy. This neediness perpetuates the cycle of accepting unwanted strokes, and the depletion continues. I teach clients to filter out such dubious offers. I call this teaching my clients to learn hesitancy. I teach them to pause before they automatically accept an offer. This gives them the opportunity to ask themselves, "Is this something I need or want?" Hesitation is a preparation for graciously saying, "I appreciate the thought, but no thanks." Unlike Snow White, clients can say to themselves, "Should I be suspicious of this offer?" In this way, to go back to our fairy tale, clients can learn to reject the poisoned apple.

From my perspective as a psychotherapist, there are a few rules about when to accept and when to reject strokes. I encourage clients to reject positive strokes that don't feel honest or genuine, or if they create pressure for the client to do something they don't want to do. I also encourage clients to analyze and reject negative strokes that are unnecessarily painful.

The processes of a stroke economy that I have described are interactive. They are the experiences we have with others that help us maintain an emotional balance sheet. The final seven actions in the stroke economy are internal. If you were managing a department store, you would call these in-house procedures. Marking down and marking up are two actions that most clearly show clients how to be in charge of their own emotional economies and to feel empowered.

Case 17: Julie

Clients have the ability to minimize the emotional effects of negative strokes by marking down. Twelve-year-old Julie's mother brought her to see me because Julie was severely depressed. According to her mother, she'd recently had a falling out with her best friend. We spent a session reviewing what Julie called "the big fight," which was over a boy.

"What happened in the big fight?" I asked.

Julie said, "My closest friend, Sue Ann, hates me. That's what she said during our awful fight."

"Do you hate Sue Ann?" I asked.

"No," she answered, "but my feelings are trashed."

"Did you say anything that might have hurt her feelings?" I asked.

"Well … I said, 'He thinks I'm prettier and nicer.'"

"Do you suppose her feelings were hurt by that?"

"I don't know," Julie pouted.

"Would it have hurt your feelings if she had said that about you?"

"Yes, but not nearly as much as the hate thing."

I explained the idea of strokes to her. We talked about how during fights, especially with friends, we tend to feel the strokes of others more intensely. We may find out after that intense experience that they were not as important as we thought, and that we can mark down their importance in our own minds.

I used a 1 to 10 scale, much like that used for pain, to ask Julie how negative she felt the stroke was. I said, "Let's say that 10 is the most negative stroke you can get, and it's terrible. A 1 is a very mild stroke and it's not very upsetting," I continued. "Your job is to decide where this stroke belongs on the scale of 1 to 10, so you know how important it really is to you."

I sent Julie off to do her homework, and when she came in the next week she reported, "My friend doesn't really hate me, but we're not best friends either."

As Julie learned about giving and getting strokes, she was able, with my help, to mark them up and down. Strokes fluctuated in their importance over a period of 2 months. The two girls became best friends again, and were able to begin exchanging positive strokes, which is one of the benefits of a best friend. Julie's depression disappeared over time.

We can mark up positive strokes just as we mark up negative strokes. I often help clients mark up positives strokes to enhance their sense of self-worth. A classic example of providing both positive and negative strokes is a performance evaluation, which lets supervisors give both positive and negative strokes to improve employee performance. A good evaluation includes a positive comment first, constructive criticism next, and a final positive comment. The bitter taste of the criticism, even though merited, has been surrounded by positive strokes and will be more acceptable.

When done well, performance evaluations can actually help people mark up their self-esteem twice. When positive comments in the evaluation are shared with an employee by the supervisor, it's a stroke for the employee. When they are again shared with the supervisor's manager, they again provide positive strokes. Not everyone values strokes the same way. A colleague in training with me related to me that her training supervisor told her, "You have an exceptional ability to listen and stay out of a client's way." To the training supervisor, that was only a $10 stroke. But my colleague marked it up to $100 in solid gold and has realized the value of staying out of clients' ways and letting *them* do the work.

Modifying strokes can take their power a step further. We can actually accept a negative stroke, reduce its negativity, and use the lesson contained in it to our benefit. It's a way of helping clients see events in an entirely different way.

Case 18: Brian

This is what happened with Brian, a college student whom I saw in therapy. He was devastated when his high school sweetheart broke off their relationship 4 months into his first year in college. She had begun dating someone else, and he was extremely hurt and angry, heaping many negative strokes on her and on himself.

Our review of the relationship helped Brian realize how young they both were. Over time they had made a commitment to each other. Over time, he began to see the initial negative stroke, the breakup, as a positive event. He acknowledged that it had prevented a relationship that would not have been satisfying for either of them. The negative stroke became, modified, a positive experience. Brian soon began dating other women.

Another way of controlling a stroke economy is the ability to self-stroke. Have you ever finished a task, reviewed it, and said to yourself, "I did a pretty good job on that"? Congratulations! You just gave yourself a positive stroke. Or say you are feeling down, and decide to give yourself a pep talk. This self-stroking is a good way to keep your stroke economy active, and it makes you less dependent on strokes from other people.

We can also make ourselves feel bad with negative self-stroking, using phrases such as "I can't do anything right," or "I screwed up again," or "I'll never be able to do that." These are self-defeating negative strokes. And if we are capable of negative self-strokes, we are also capable of positive self-stroking.

Another thing we can do with strokes, even if we collected them a long time ago, is to reactivate or remember them. These may be strokes that have lost their value over time. Suppose that one day, you are going through files to do some purging. You find a playbill and a note from the director of a community theater for a performance you starred in 30 years ago. You'd forgotten all about it, but finding the playbill and the note reactivates the whole experience for you—the stage, the acting, the applause. Those strokes have again become a significant and active part of your stroke economy.

Reactivation can happen spontaneously through memories of happy experiences. Such reactivation is a valuable therapeutic tool that I use with clients. Likewise, even the reactivation of negative experiences during psychotherapy can give clients a chance to revisit sad experiences and modify their feelings about them.

Case 19: "Horse"

The story of "Horse," a Vietnam veteran who I was treating for depression and anxiety, demonstrates how strokes can be reactivated years later. Horse claimed that nothing had happened to make him depressed or anxious. I suspected posttraumatic stress disorder (PTSD) but Horse rejected that idea.

Several sessions into his therapy, he told me that he had been watching a TV show about Vietnam, something he almost never did. Indeed, he avoided conversations about Vietnam whenever he could. The program showed some of the tunnels that the Vietnamese used for transportation, storage, and shelter. Horse said, "I remembered getting ready to blow up a tunnel." He was surprised to recall the incident and skeptical when I suggested that his Vietnam experience might have a part in his depression and anxiety. After more psychotherapy, which reactivated his long-repressed and painful feelings, we were able to get to the source of his depression and treat it.

The stroke economy concept offers a number of other possibilities for psychotherapy. We can use it to condition clients to be more alert, sensitive, and interpersonally active in sharing with their significant others. The Stroke Economy Worksheet below is an easy-to-use tool for applying the principles of the stroke economy. I use these worksheets like a bank statement to show my clients the condition of their account. Like a bank statement, the worksheet makes connections between spending and saving.

Here are two questions I include as I discuss strokes with clients:

> Do I (we) have as much currency (positive strokes) in our account as we want or need? (Doesn't it go without question that we should have enough in our account to weather storms?)

Are we regularly banking more positives and not making unnecessary withdrawals? Standard withdrawals might take the form of quarrels, bickering, fighting, neglect, indifference, and sarcasm.

A worksheet such as the one shown above, kept and reviewed regularly, will help clients review their emotional portfolios and will provide the feedback they need to make positive changes (see Figure 4.2).

Today, most psychotherapy approaches are symptom-driven. They're a "fix" for something that is broken. But the stroke economy has broader parameters. It can open frontiers for prevention much like those currently in play in public health. Incorporated into clients' daily lives and habits, a stroke economy can be preventive. A banker doesn't let you drain your portfolio. Rather, he or she guides you, makes suggestions, and shows you how to read the balance sheet and maintain a healthy investment balance. So should it be with an emotional portfolio. With guidance, clients can maintain a healthy balance sheet and enjoy an emotionally full and healthy life.

DEPOSITS

Did you do something special this month to strengthen the relationship?

If Yes, enter the # of items times 1.0

If No, enter 0

Did you do some little thing on a daily basis to let your partner/spouse know that you were thinking of them?

If Yes, add .5 per day times the # of days

If No, enter 0

Total Monthly Deposits_______

WITHDRAWALS

Did you say or do something that hurt your partner's/spouse's feelings?

If Yes , enter # of items times x 2.0

If No, enter 0

Did you say or do something that was cross/disappointing?

If Yes, enter # of items times x 1.0

Total Monthly Withdrawals_______

Note: Hurtful behavior or comments tend to have much more impact on the relationship than positive behavior.

Summary from Previous Month's EP (Emotional Portfol io)

This Month's Deposits_______

This Month's Withdrawals_______

Emotional Balance________

Figure 4.2 Worksheet I—Couples'/Partners' Emotional Bank Account Monthly Statement.

5 The Psychotherapist as Artist

> A picture lives a life like a living creature, undergoing changes imposed on us by our lives, from day to day. This is natural enough, as the picture lives only through the man who is looking at it.
>
> (Pablo Picasso, O'Brian, 1976, p. 1510)

Artists often later rework a picture that they have apparently finished. In 1906, Picasso started a painting. An early sketch showed a sailor sitting with a group of nude women with fruit and flowers at his feet. But when the painting, *Demoiselles d'Avignon*, was completed in the spring of 1907, the sailor was no longer there. Picasso had removed an element of the composition and changed the focus of the painting.

Artists may repaint a picture many times, taking objects out, putting elements in, changing colors or textures. One of the most important insights that the psychotherapist can gain from the artist and use in his or her therapeutic work, is that we don't always have to see a scene in the same way. Monet, for example, produced 30 pictures of Rouen Cathedral, clearly showing us that one can see the same thing in many different ways.

The psychotherapist who functions as an artist can employ at least four artistic techniques with clients. The first is to create a psychological canvas based on the specific information that the client provides. Content may come from the client's current life, previous experience, or dream states. It can also come from clients' personal values and their wishes for the future. This gives the psychotherapist a wide array of subject matter for his or her canvas. Usually, the resulting picture is based on the specific problems that the client brings to the therapy. It's the way the client pictures his or her current life or life in the recent past.

The second technique is to help the client picture both the content and the emotions that they are dealing with. The third function is to teach clients the different ways scenes can be depicted. The fourth is to encourage them to create their own canvases, pictures that will depict their lives as they want them to be.

Functioning much as an artist, the psychotherapist can show the client how it might be possible to see a painful, frightening event in a different light, or from new perspectives, over the course of therapy. Thus the same event can move from traumatizing to informative or even comforting.

George Cherepov, author of *Discovering Oil Painting* (1971), notes that there are five elements of a painting that can drastically modify the picture (p. 25). I'd like to review three of them: subject, perspective, and color. These elements can be used by the psychotherapist much as they are used by an artist.

Cherepov says: "First, analyze the subject you intend to paint and try to find out which part you consider most important" (1999, p. 31). As a trained psychotherapist, I often function as an artist does, focusing on a particular subject. Clients will usually tell me about the events that color and shape their outlook on life. Often, through the course of therapy, their perception changes several times, thereby altering the painting.

Case 20: Penny

Penny consulted me because she was concerned about the poor school performance of her 14-year-old daughter, Jennifer. As we began to talk, I noticed how beautifully Penny was dressed. She wore a slim black dress, a necklace of glistening African beads, and a hand-painted shawl. The effect was fashionably artistic, which was not surprising because Penny was the well-respected owner of an art gallery and an antique shop. She had a reputation as a sophisticated and successful woman. Her family had left her an estate, and her husband owned an architectural firm. I felt that using the visual approach of the psychotherapist as an artist might resonate with her.

Her opening statement was, "My husband and I had a terrible fight last night. I thought it was about our daughter's indifference to school. But I'm not so sure he wasn't mad about my extravagance." Although Penny's stated reason for seeing me were her daughter's grades and apparent lack of motivation, the focus during our first session was almost exclusively on Penny. I learned about her busy work schedule, her gallery, and her husband's career and business connections. Her life was the picture of success.

I also learned about her shopping habit. According to her husband, she consistently overspent on clothes, accessories, purses, and other things she didn't need, and this overspending was creating tension between the two of them. She admitted to me that her closet was crammed with clothes and shoes she had never worn, and she said she shopped just as compulsively for Jennifer, whose own closets were stuffed with unworn clothing.

Penny lit up as she told me about the things she bought, and how pleasurable she found it to shop, either online or in specialty boutiques. But when I asked her about her home life and her marriage, her mood dampened. She described her husband Clark as a workaholic, who, in her words, "Even when he's home, he's not really there." She described as happy the many hours while her daughter was in school that she spent shopping.

It became clear to me that Penny shopped out of loneliness. As the tension between Penny and her husband became worse, she shopped out of frustration and defiance, as well.

As Penny revealed these behaviors to me over several sessions, I developed a "sketch" with Penny in the foreground, surrounded by several overfull closets of stuff that no longer made her happy. There did not seem to be room for her husband or daughter in the picture we were developing together.

While Penny was in therapy with me, Jennifer got arrested for shoplifting, and that put her in the foreground of the evolving painting. Penny began to realize that her shopping habit created tension in the family and perhaps even contributed to her daughter's behaviors—the acting out and the shoplifting.

My role as a psychotherapist was to help Penny redraw the picture that she was describing to me, and to change the picture as her focus on what was important to her shifted. I was able to help Penny identify aspects of her life that she had neglected, including her daughter's emotional needs.

One of the pictures I drew for her was Jennifer's near-frantic reaction when she overheard the many fights between her parents. One might think that Jennifer's reaction to these fights would have been obvious to Penny, but when she was in the middle of a battle, she was oblivious to Jennifer's feelings.

As Penny started paying more attention to Jennifer, the fears that Jennifer had experienced began appearing on the canvas. Would her parents divorce? Would she have to change schools? Would her father leave? Penny asked me whether she should bring her daughter in to see me, but I encouraged her to reach out to Jennifer in reassuring ways on her own. I felt that this would be a way for Penny to participate in painting her own canvas, one that included Jennifer.

Over time, Penny started spending more time with her daughter, and less time shopping. She started to review Jennifer's homework and make sure she finished her assignments on time. According to Penny, Jennifer's resentment of what she had called Penny's "interference" subsided. Both she and Jennifer found their time together reviewing homework pleasant. Jennifer's grades improved and she stopped acting out at school. At my final session with Penny, she told me that her family was doing well.

The picture that I had developed with Penny changed radically during our sessions together. Instead of a lone, elegant figure of a woman in a slim black dress and artistic jewelry, the canvas became one of a mother and daughter, hand in hand. While her husband, Clark, still didn't figure prominently in the picture, Penny was coping with his workaholism and the fights had almost been eliminated.

Case 21: Georgie and Tommy

Here is another story in which I was able first to draw a picture to show the client and his worried mother, and then repaint it several times. It was apparent from my first encounter with this harried mother, Georgie and her 11-year-old son, Tommy what the problem was, and it was quite odiferous. With much embarrassment, she told me that her son "messed in his pants" every day, sometimes several times a day when he was home watching television. He didn't have this problem at school, so I knew that he had sphincter control.

She had consulted a pediatrician, who told Georgie that there was nothing physically wrong with Tommy. She contacted me, hoping that therapy would help solve Tommy's encopresis. When she and I first met, she said, "Everyone is telling me that this is an emotional problem. He's angry and hurt because his father and I divorced." She continued, "Tommy's father left when he was one, and Tommy has no memory of him." Georgie told me that she knew it would take a long time and a lot of sessions to uncover the actual cause of Tommy's behavior and help him overcome it. She assumed that Tommy and I would spend years getting to the heart of his problem.

Georgie and Tommy began regular weekly sessions with me. The first picture we drew together featured Georgie's shame, anger, and embarrassment. It was a sharp contrast to Tommy's indifference to his problem.

To Tommy's delight, I sketched a picture of his encopresis, and we called it "Mr. Poop." By separating his condition from his mother's feelings about it, I thought I could help Tommy address the problem. As I began asking Tommy and his mother about Mr. Poop's appearances, Tommy described him for me as a dirty little man dressed in brown. He showed up, uninvited, and always surprised Tommy in the afternoon after he got home from school. "I'm just watching TV, and there he is!" said Tommy.

Because I needed to know what was triggering the encopresis, I gave Tommy an assignment between sessions to be on the lookout for Mr. Poop, and to tell me during the next session when Mr. Poop showed up, and what he, Tommy, was doing at the time. I also asked him to take care of Mr. Poop—to clean up himself and the bathroom, and then wash and dry the soiled clothing. He wasn't so happy about the laundry part of the assignment—his mother had been handling it up to now—but he agreed to do it. I also asked Georgie to reward Tommy each time he took care of Mr. Poop's messes.

During our second session, Tommy told me that Mr. Poop usually appeared an hour or so after he got home from school. Now his mother would come home from work and find the washing machine running. Tommy even missed part of his TV shows to get his laundry done. Just as he had described Mr. Poop to me in the beginning, he now began to describe the washing machine and the clean clothes, and his smile reflected his pride in looking after himself and making his mother happy. I changed the picture accordingly, with Mr. Poop very much in the background, as Tommy said, "Ah, he's not as important as he was."

For the next several weeks, I gave Tommy a new task: to try to beat Mr. Poop to the punch, and go to the bathroom and poop (now an action verb, not a noun.) He agreed to this cheerfully and told me all about it the next week. He was surprised only twice by Mr. Poop, once on Saturday while watching TV, and once on Sunday, when he and his mom were having lunch with his aunts.

Tommy learned after both of these incidents that Mr. Poop could still surprise us, but Mr. Poop was becoming less dominant in our drawing, and Tommy described the washing machine and dryer as enthusiastically as he had previously described Mr. Poop.

Georgie was encouraged. She liked the new painting and as Mr. Poop diminished in importance and size, she became more relaxed and seemed less harried.

The following week, Mr. Poop didn't show up. I praised Tommy for getting the best of Mr. Poop and told him to keep working his program because Mr. Poop was a sly one and wouldn't give up his surprises easily. He agreed to keep working at the task, and his mom, who was almost in a state of shocked disbelief, agreed to help him. After all, she had anticipated years of psychotherapy for Tommy.

We erased Mr. Poop from our picture. When I checked a week later, I learned that Mr. Poop hadn't been up to his old tricks, and a session 2 weeks later revealed continued success. We continued to meet on an as-needed basis. I did talk to Georgie 3 months later, just before Thanksgiving—a holiday laden with feelings about food and family—and I was pleased to learn that Mr. Poop had not shown up. Case closed on Mr. Poop.

Some of my colleagues may wonder why I didn't address the anger that Tommy's mother assumed he had. Seeing no sign of that anger, I chose not to focus on it. The behavior had been changed, and Tommy seemed happy. Georgie worried that Tommy's encopresis might return. I reassured her that if it did, she and Tommy would know what to do.

Tommy's case was actually closed 2½ years ago. About a year ago, curious about how Tommy was doing, I called Georgie. I was not really surprised to learn that Tommy's encopresis had become an occasional problem, but for the most part, Mr. Poop was out of the picture. Tommy and I had created and then erased a visual picture of Tommy's problem.

Paul Cézanne, the French Post-Impressionist painter, suggested that if we view a scene or object first with one eye, and then the other, the view changes. As a psychotherapist, I sometimes adapt Cezanne's approach by helping clients see traumatic events "with the other eye"; that is, in a different way. I have found Cezanne's suggestion helpful over the years as I treat veterans with PTSD. Such clients talk about firefights and the horrors of picking up the bodies and body parts of their comrades. They are haunted by their experiences and can't let go of the memories, which come back to them in flashbacks.

Case 22: Hank

Hank was a tall, rangy young man of 23 who had served two tours in Iraq. His Southern roots were evident in his accent and in his manners. He had only been discharged a few months before I first saw him. Referred through his employer, Hank was having trouble concentrating, which was affecting his job performance. His general demeanor was apologetic. He explained that he would offer someone a cup of coffee, spill a bit in the saucer, hand it to them, and say, "I'm sorry." Handing a coworker a memo, he'd drop it and say, "I'm sorry." He told me that one of his colleagues told him he was the sorriest man she knew.

The first canvas that I helped Hank paint depicted his current situation. It showed an inattentive Hank lying awake at night for reasons he couldn't really pin down. He said, "Thoughts just keep racing through my mind."

I asked him to keep a log of his thoughts, and to spend a couple of minutes jotting down the highlights of what he was visualizing when those thoughts raced through his mind. He and I were looking for a focal point for the canvas we were painting. I also asked him to keep a dream log. He had been having nightmares, but thought they were inconsequential. One frequently recurring nightmare was that of his father stepping off the curb into a busy street. "What happened?" I asked. "Nothing," he said. "But I was sure there would have been an accident if I hadn't pulled him back to the curb. And when I pulled him back," Hank went on, "I apologized to him over and over again."

Many of Hank's dreams were about impending accidents, or accidents that could have happened. Often he was in a position to intervene. The emerging canvas we were painting showed him in the foreground, actively preventing accidents, and lying awake afterwards, shocked by the experience and asking, "What if I hadn't yelled?" Even in his dreams, he was constantly apologizing to people he had saved. "I'm sorry, I'm sorry," he'd repeat in the dream, and then he'd lie awake apologizing.

After several sessions, I asked Hank to recall a real-life situation in which he could have perhaps made a difference by intervening, but had failed to do so. He hesitated before responding, looking down at his lap and shaking his head, as if to wipe away a memory. He spoke with sadness and regret in his voice.

"Here's a situation that I really do feel guilty about. I should have done something, and I didn't." He spoke quietly, gazing down at the floor, his arms wrapped around his lean frame. He told me a war story. He had been on a patrol heading toward a location where insurgents were blocking the road. Prepared for a firefight, his reinforced squad arrived, only to find that the enemy had been there and left. They established a command post in the area, holding ground in the event the enemy returned. When they got orders to evacuate, they left in two Humvees. Bumping across the desolate, sandy landscape, the first Humvee, in which Hank was riding shotgun, hit an IED. When Hank and the others got enough sand out of their eyes to look around, they discovered that the driver was unconscious and that his foot had been blown off by the explosives. They put a tourniquet on the stump of his leg and placed the foot, still in its boot, on his chest. Hank called for help, and he and the rest of the squad waited until the driver was helicoptered out.

As Hank recounted this story, he described the driver's boot, with his foot still in it, poking out of the remains of the Humvee. As Hank spoke, he experienced a painful flashback. His face turned pale, his hands shook, and he was gasping for breath. As we painted this canvas I said, "This is a pretty clear picture you're painting. Can you remember what went through your mind after this happened?" He took a deep breath. "I felt guilty. I felt that I should have been seen the IED. It was my fault. I felt ashamed. I really mean it when I said, 'I'm sorry' in my dreams. I could have kept this from happening."

This was Hank's "Sorry" painting, with the bloody boot at the center of the canvas. Using what I called the "Cezanne view," I helped Hank view the incident another way. I suggested that he imagine the alternative scenario, where he was driving. He realized that the boot would have contained his foot. He recognized that he had acted responsibly. He had nothing to apologize for. As with other case histories in this chapter, a visual depiction of the traumatic event, and a revision of that depiction, was the key to helping clients heal from trauma and anxiety.

Over time, Hank's guilt dissipated. While his PTSD did not completely disappear, he was functioning better and felt that he could handle his job and his life. Not too long after our sessions ended, Hank quit feeling guilty about everything and stopped apologizing, although, as he said, apologetically, "It's a hard habit to break."

Color is another of the artist's tools that the therapist can add to his or her therapeutic palate. According to Picasso biographer Patrick

O'Brian, Picasso's color palate became predominantly blue in the summer of 1901, when Picasso was into a stage that would later be called his Blue Period. The shift in palate was in response to the suicide of his friend, fellow artist Carlos Casagemas (O'Brien, 1976). The Blue Period came to an end 3 years later, when Picasso met Fernande Olivier, who became first his mistress and later his wife. He began using pink, employing color to describe his universe and all that was in it. From a depressed blue, Picasso then moved to excited and optimistic pink hues, reflecting his changing state of mind (O'Brien, 1976).

By encouraging clients to identify their current, past, and desired future color palettes it is possible to help them change the colors of their "life palettes." What I am suggesting is that behaviors can be changed by how people view their world. Just as we change behavior by changing feelings, and vice versa, we can change behaviors or feelings by changing our perception of them.

Colors are commonly used to express feelings. We say, "She has the blues," "He saw red," or "She looks at the world through rose-colored glasses." In much the same way that an artist changes color to create mood, with guidance clients have the capacity to paint over old canvases of sadness, regret, disappointment, and guilt.

Case 23: Laura

I once treated a woman in her 80s, Laura, who had painted small landscapes on and off during her life. Her children, grandchildren, and a number of her friends owned her pictures, usually of the farm and countryside where she had lived most of her life. But after her husband died, she had to move into the city to be closer to one of her children, and she no longer painted. When I saw her, she hadn't painted in more than 2 years. She was depressed and felt her life was over.

Laura knew I was interested in art, and had noticed the art books in my office, so she agreed to bring in a couple of her paintings and tell me about them. Her paintings were bright, cheerful, and pleasantly primitive. They were filled with the vibrant greens of spring, the warm yellows and browns of the fall harvest, the brilliantly shining snow covering the fields in winter. As she described the time and events reflected in each of the pictures, she became revitalized.

I gave Laura the therapeutic task of painting again, pointing out to her how much showing and talking about her previous work had cheered her up. She resisted the idea, but I urged her to get her easel and paints out of storage and give painting another try. She did, first producing several new "old farm" pictures, which didn't please her. "I don't have a feel for it," she complained. I suggested that she try to paint city scenes. Slowly at first, but with increasing interest, she admitted that she was seeing and learning to appreciate the colors and sights of the city.

"Have you ever noticed how bright and demanding the reds and greens of the traffic lights are?" she asked me, smiling. Her artist's eye had been awakened; she was again engaged, and some of her joy in life was back. During our time together, she periodically brought in snapshots of her works in progress. Her paintings became steadily brighter, as did her affect. She had painted her way out of depression. Changing the subject, the perspective, and color of a memory are just three of the artist's techniques that a psychotherapist can use to bring about effective change.

The artist also brings another concept to psychotherapy. I call it "project time"—which describes how long a task, say a painting, is "worked on" before the artist is done with it. Please note that I didn't say "finished," because for some artists, the painting always need more work.

For Leonardo da Vinci, the perfection of the Mona Lisa was probably a lifetime pursuit. Art historians usually list it as being painted from 1503 to 1515. In truth, da Vinci left a great number of his paintings unfinished. Much of his art remained works-in-progress for long periods of time. Or consider the panels that Giotto de Bondone (1267–1337) painted for the Arena Chapel in Padua. He worked *buon fresco*, which means the colors are infused into the wet plaster. When the plaster dries, the work is finished. In Italian, a section is called *giornata,* or "a day's work."

Monet provides yet another example of project time. While he was creating the paintings of the Rouen Cathedral, he was in temporarily rented second-floor space just across the street, working on each piece in the series of 30 paintings for a few minutes at a time, when the light was just right. Perhaps some of psychotherapeutic work should be for 20 minutes or less, or maybe even just once a month. Each case is unique.

At the opposite end of the spectrum are marathon-type sessions. I recall a sensitivity training "marathon" I attended. It lasted 48 hours nonstop. After about 6 hours straight, it became for me a very dynamic and emotional experience. After about 24 hours, my defenses (and I believe everyone else's) were worn completely down. I couldn't help but be absolutely direct and open. I remember thinking, with tears streaming down my face, "I love the whole human race." (By the next day I had recovered from this typical reaction.)

I'm not suggesting that clients should subject themselves to marathons of this sort, but I am proposing again that we question the "project time" needed in psychotherapy. Perhaps the 50-minute hour once or twice a week is not the most effective time frame for psychotherapeutic change. It may, in fact, be a residual feature of psychoanalysis—with its deep probing of repressed or suppressed emotions—which is not suited to the more solution-oriented strategic therapy I've been describing. There are some psychotherapists who work very rapidly, in small increments in time. Milton Erickson's single-session hypnotic work is an example. In

Uncommon Therapy, famed therapist Jay Haley (1973/1999) describes Erickson's astonishingly quick psychotherapies: "Erickson tends to focus upon the specific presenting problem and to resolve it in the most efficient and economical manner (Haley, 1986, p. 230) There's really no right or wrong project time, but being flexible about it can be to the client's benefit.

These few examples compare the long, slow never-finished work to the quick work of the *buon fresco*. They compare short periods of activity in exactly the right environment to the intense experience of the marathon sensitivity session. As in art, psychotherapy is, for some clients, a work-in-progress for a long time. For others, the results are quickly achieved. It's the responsibility of the psychotherapist to know which technique will work for any given client. It is interesting to consider the progress and project time of psychotherapy as an analogy to project time in art, and may provide more options for clients. It gives the psychotherapist the choice of putting aside the usual idea of psychotherapeutic time constraints and focusing on the work at hand.

Art gives us another lens through which to view psychotherapy, and it may very well be one that preserves the inherent human ability and desire for creativity in all its forms. In *Painting as a Language* (2000), the authors, Jean Robertson and Craig McDaniel, point out that "As society rushes headlong into the future and the cultural landscape appears to be increasingly dominated by modes of electronic communication, the practice of painting remains a vital endeavor. As a painter, you are engaged in freedom of thought and bodily movement, a heightened awareness of sensory input and sensual textures, an unlimited opportunity for emotional expression and the exploration of a captivating means of communication that stretches back to the dawn of human history" (p. 10). Just as art mirrors life, so can psychotherapy, providing options for clients to visually express their feelings and actually alter their memories of traumatic events. The concept of a psychotherapist as an artist can serve many clients well, and may provide a future direction for psychotherapy.

6 The Psychotherapist as Engineer

I recently came across a definition of a chemical engineer in "Chemical Engineer," a pamphlet in a career series that explains that chemical engineers "take measurements on ... temperature, pressure, density and other properties ..." (Chemical Engineer, 2003, p. 1). In my mind, it doesn't take a huge stretch of imagination to conceive of human beings in engineering terms—with the body as a chemical plant and the brain as the instrument responsible for measuring and controlling the body's functions. Thus we can think of the psychotherapist as an engineer.

People often describe emotions metaphorically as liquids: "Her sorrow overflowed," "His feelings were all damned up," "She cried a river of tears," "His feelings were like a bottomless lake," "A tidal wave of emotion hit her." This observation has led me to consider a psychotherapy model based on engineering. Assume for a moment "optimism training"—a phrase first coined by psychologist Martin Seligman—as a way to store positive affect. In *Learned Optimism: How to Change Your Mind and Your Life*, Seligman emphasized the importance of "learning a set of skills about how to talk to *yourself* when you suffer a defeat. You will learn to speak to yourself about your setbacks from a more encouraging viewpoint" (Seligman, 1998, p. 290).

If we think of affect as a liquid, then we must have a system to generate good feelings. Once we have generated those feelings, we can identify, access, process, filter, store, and utilize them.

In this chapter I explain how psychotherapists can adapt the activities of an engineer to help clients manage their feelings. The Affect Gauge and the Affect Chart show how this process works.

The charts have three primary components. The Affect Gauge is an indicator of the positive affect (emotional resources) that an individual has available. Much like a gauge on an automobile, if it indicates that the person is well-supplied with positive affect, the gauge will read "comfort." If he or she is running low on affect, for instance in the bottom quarter of the gauge, the gauge will read "caution." Should the gauge reach the bottom, the person is facing crisis or collapse, "running on empty." This is the gauge that the psychotherapist as engineer uses to

Affect Gauge

Comfort

Joy,
Happiness,
Contentment,
Excitement,
Desire to Do More,
Energy,
Enthusiasm

Caution

Discomfort,
Discouraged,
Irritable,
Fatigue,
Self Doubts,
Anger,
Worry,
Frustration

Crisis and Collapse

Pain,
Depressed,
Fearful,
Anxious,
Some Rage,
Dread,
Very Pessimistic
Panic,
Hospitalized,
Severe Depression,
Physical Breakdown

Figure 6.1 Affect Gauge.

assess the client's available emotional resources and to determine how close the client is to emotional collapse.

The second chart can be used to help the client build emotional reserves and conserve those resources. It is essentially a list of therapeutic activities that can help the client generate and conserve positive affect—in other words, to fill the tank. Psychotherapy both helps clients generate positive affect and teaches them to conserve it.

Using this chart as a guide, the psychotherapist can help clients learn to manage their emotional needs, and to monitor the activities they use to fill their affect tanks. The case histories that follow demonstrate how these activities—generating, identifying, accessing, processing, filtering, storing, and utilizing positive affect—can improve the lives of clients.

Generate Positive Affect	Conservation of Affect
1. Increase Social Networking • Supportive System Review and Improve • Stroke Economy Training • Power Training • Social Network Training **2. Communication Skill Building** • Communication Training • Conflict Management • Active Listening **3. Self Awareness training** • Self Awareness Training • Self Acceptance Training • Goal Setting • Belief and Value System "Find out what's important to you" • Meditation **4. Increasing Joys and Pleasures** • Develop a "Want List" • Giving Yourself Permission or Attend Permission Classes • Play, Pleasure, Fun **5. Constructive Mental Attitude Training** • Learn Constructive Worrying • Develop Positive Expectations	**1. Developing More Effective Coping Skills** • Assertiveness Training • Active Listening • Conflict Resolution Skills **2. Avoid Gaming Behaviors** • Game Analysis • Avoiding Discounts • Avoid the Rescue Triangle • Avoid Power Plays • Script Work **3. Desensitization Training** • Reducing Fears • Reducing Angers • Reducing Frustrations • Reworking Guilt Feelings • Reducing Doubling and Insecurity **4. Productive Skills Training** • Time Management and Pacing • Planning and Organizing • Decision Making • Prioritizing • Delegation • Supervision **5. Stress Reduction Techniques-Training** • Breathing Exercises • Relaxation Techniques • Autogenic training • Meditation Training • Psycho-Imagery • Visualization Training • Practice Surrender Control • Worry Workshop

Figure 6.2 Affect Generation and Conservation Chart.

For most clients, like Joyce, whose story follows, it's necessary to first build reserves, and then to guide them to conserve those reserves.

Case 24: Joyce

About 3 years ago Joyce, a woman in her 20s, came into my office. She said, "I know I'm seriously depressed, but I don't know why. I have low energy; I cry a lot; I'm unmotivated. I have trouble sleeping and I've lost my appetite. I'm a college graduate and I have a job as an associate editor that pays well. And I have a reasonably steady love life. So it surprises me that I'm depressed and so uninspired to do anything about it."

I asked her to define a "reasonably steady love life," since this didn't sound very satisfying to me. She described it as being like ocean tides, flowing in and out. She said that she had been dating her boyfriend, Henry, for 2 years. They had reached a point where both felt taken for granted.

"Sometimes I'm angry at him when he has done nothing to deserve it, and I'm pushing him away. Other times, I'm completely happy with him when he hasn't actually done anything different. He says he loves the good times and is confused when I drive him away."

Using her metaphor, I asked her first to chart these events as if they were tides. I explained to her that people who live near the ocean know when tides will be in, high tide, and out, low tide. I showed her a tidal chart. I suggested that she record when and how her personal emotional tides fluctuated, hoping it might help her understand and modify her behavior. I knew from experience that any time a client is able to log or chart their feelings, it can bring them emotional understanding and control.

This approach incorporates the principles of cognitive behavioral therapy. As defined on the Cognitive Behavioral Therapy Academy's website, "Cognitive Therapy is a focused, problem-solving psychotherapy that has been shown in over 400 outcome studies to be highly effective for the treatment of many mental health problems such as depression, general anxiety disorders, panic, and marital distress. It has also been shown to be effective for the treatment of medical conditions such as chronic pain, hypertension, and fibromyalgia. The therapist and client work together as a team to identify and solve problems, and therapists help clients to overcome the anxieties through changing their thinking, behavior, and emotional response" (Academy of Cognitive Therapy, n.d.).

I asked Joyce to list her complaints about the relationship. My goal was to help her learn what she was actually upset about and to explore whether her reactions were valid. I wanted to get an overall picture of where there was excessive pressure, so that I could help Joyce identify those pressure points and decide which of them could be remedied.

Joyce identified, to her own surprise, Henry's dirty fingernails as a real annoyance. There were other annoyances, too. Some, like the fingernail problem, were easily solved. When I saw Henry alone, I asked him to consider how important appearances were to Joyce, and asked him whether he thought that trimming and cleaning his nails would please her. Henry agreed to this, and said, laughing, "If I clean my nails will that get her off my back?" "Probably not completely," I answered, "but it will show her that you are trying to make things better."

An important benefit of the annoyance list was that it gave Joyce, who didn't know why she was so upset with Henry, specifics that they could address together. This in turn gave her a chance to choose which annoyances could be easily and quickly corrected; which could be modified over time to a point where they were acceptable; and those that were not correctable and were destined for a long-term waste tank discharged by her as unnecessary.

These engineering metaphors helped enhance and support the cognitive therapy principles by giving Joyce concrete physical concepts to think about. With the affect charting, Joyce finally recognized that the high tides of annoyance were related to her menstrual cycle. This helped her recognize when she might be more sensitive to small annoyances so that she and Henry could ride out these episodes together.

When I asked Joyce what she and Henry were doing to strengthen the relationship, I got a blank stare. So I knew they needed help in this respect. I asked each of them separately to make another list, this time of things they could do to strengthen the relationship. I gave them suggestions to get them started: Quality time-sharing, small romantic surprises, or a special act of thoughtfulness. I suggested that they write love notes to one another. And I asked them to write down what they had done for each other. I explained to them that strengthening the relationship through these small efforts was like reinforcing the storage tank of her affect so that it could handle more pressure.

I was helping Joyce and Henry by using procedures that an engineer might employ. I was using charts and lists to record and interpret data; I was encouraging Joyce to check the pressure in her affect tank, and helping her learn how to create a more positive affect so that she would have reserves under pressure. I was helping Joyce monitor her satisfaction and stress levels proactively.

All of these efforts—the lists, the charting, and the repair work—made Joyce feel that she had some control over her emotions. We continued to chart and graph, and we used the charts and graphs for reference as we worked together. Several weeks later, she told me that Henry had commented that their relationship was more loving and less antagonistic. Joyce was reassured that we were on the right track.

It was about a month later that she discovered from the chart that in addition to the times when she had her period, there were peaks of discontent that correlated with the times at work when almost everyone was out of the office. At first she had appreciated the quiet time to catch up on work, but now she acknowledged that after a few days of being alone in the office, she became lonely. She would then go home feeling "demanding and crabby," in her words, which drove Henry away and made her feel even worse. The empty feeling she described was so acute that we began a "Loneliness Chart," which made her realize that she was painfully lonely. We used the standard 10-point pain scale, with 1 being "not lonely at all," and 10 being "as miserably lonely as a person can be." As the chart displayed over time, it was clear that she needed a certain level of social interaction to avoid being lonely and depressed.

She began to spend more time with her family and friends. She admitted that when her relationship with Henry was first developing, she had seriously neglected the rest of her social network. She developed a plan to rekindle her friendships, and she soon discovered that some of her depressive state could be modified by the pleasure she got from social interaction.

We had another session 2 weeks later. Joyce's outlook and general affect seemed improved. A month later, she felt she was in control again and said she would call me if the problem recurred. I got a Christmas card from her 6 months later thanking me and telling me that she had stopped "charting the tides" and that she was still doing well.

Case 25: Lee

The story of Lee provides another example of the principles of engineering in psychotherapy. Several years ago, a physician referred this retired corporate executive to me. The doctor had diagnosed him with depression, put him on medication, and then suggested he see me for therapy.

Lee, a retired quality control manager, was an attractive well-dressed man in his mid-60s. He was lean, with a white mane of hair, a kind face, and a worried look. He explained to me, "My wife and doctor both think I'm depressed. I'm driving my wife crazy, because I am noticing everything that's going wrong at home. She says she can't live with a picky, critical quality control manager."

On meeting him, I didn't see the standard signs of depression. He shook my hand firmly and managed an engaging smile. He was sleeping well, his appetite was good, and he was satisfied with his life, except for his wife's discontent and his own boredom.

I gave him the Beck Depression Inventory (Beck, Ward, Mendelson, Mock, & Erbaugh, 1961) to measure his depression. He scored only a 10, which is a low score, indicating minimal depression. I asked him whether his antidepressant was effective. He told me he didn't think his antidepressant was doing any good. I suggested that perhaps he was not depressed, but had lost purpose and direction when he retired.

Lee agreed: "That's for sure! But where do I go from here?"

I suspected that there just weren't enough mental challenges in his life to keep him occupied. At work, he had had plenty of things to worry about and lots of people to order around. Now he had only his wife's household to micromanage, and she was proving difficult and unappreciative of his "help." He was only seeing me to please his wife.

Lee's problem was that he was a natural worrywart without anything to worry about. His worrying nature was part of what had made him a good quality control manager. Lee was intelligent, highly focused, and was good at paying acute attention to detail.

His house was paid for, and he had adequate savings and a comfortable lifestyle. He exercised, watched his weight, seldom drank, and didn't overeat. He was likeable, but it was clear as I talked with him that he had been a very demanding boss and a perfectionist.

As I discussed at the beginning of this chapter, positive affect—good feelings—can be saved up, in much the same way that fluids are stored in a hydraulic tank. We can reserve the good feelings we have and use them when we need them. But if the affect tank is being emptied by unconstructive worrying, as it was with Lee, it's as if there is a hole in the tank that happiness and contentment is leaking out of. My job as a psychotherapist as engineer was to help Lee learn how to direct his attention and energy constructively so that he could build up his reserves.

I showed Lee the Affect Gauge and Affect Generation and Conservation Chart that I had used with Joyce, and suggested that his gauge was reading "caution" because of the high-drain demands of his micromanaging and worrying. This concept appealed to the quality controller in him. I asked him to keep a log of his worries and concerns. The list he produced 2 weeks later was impressive in its length and scope. I suggested we call this his "worry list" and asked him to find a place that we would call his "worry office." I told him it should be an adequate space but not particularly comfortable. He needed a straight-back chair, a desk, a lamp, and file drawers for the files I had him create, one for each major worry in his life.

One of Lee's big worries was home security, so I had him set up a file called "Home Security." Every time he found himself worrying about home security, he was to make a note in his log, and then move that into the Home Security file during his selected worry time of 9:15 to 9:35 a.m. each day. I told him that was the only time he could worry. The rest of the time, he wrote his worries in his worry log, which he carried with him, and saved the worrying for the 20 minutes in the basement.

His Home Security file was eventually joined by 18 other files, all on topics he worried about. Some of them led to action, like installing a home security system. For each worry, he had an assignment: to learn more about the topic he was worrying about. This was a perfect assignment for the quality controller within.

I knew Lee was not going to stop worrying, so my solution was to help him develop tools to worry constructively. My intention was to help him maintain attention and focus so he didn't drive his wife crazy. After 3 months, his worrying evolved into productive problem solving, which helped clear his mind of worry and helped him to start experiencing more pleasure.

Six months later we discontinued therapy. His affect tank was now full. About 2 years later, I ran into his wife in the supermarket. She said, "I've been hoping to run into you, Dr. Miller, because I think you saved my marriage and my life. Lee had become increasingly impossible, and somehow, through your magic, he's become tolerable to live with." I rather liked being called a magician!

Case 26: Larry

Sometime later, Lee referred his friend Larry to me. Once again, I was able to apply the techniques of engineering to psychotherapy. Larry, a 40-something computer technician, told me he was afraid he was going to lose his job because he couldn't get along with his boss.

"Every day, he gets me so angry that my stomach turns into a knot. Whatever I say to him, whatever suggestions I make, whatever solutions I bring him, he finds a way to discount them. No matter what positive things happen around there, he manages to throw cold water on them."

I asked him to make a running list of just what his boss was doing to him and to others. The following week he brought me a list with four examples of what his boss had said to him and two things that his boss had said to fellow workers.

"It seems like your boss is attacking you more than anyone else," I observed.

"That's right; and it's not that I don't do my job. I've been working there for 7 years and have had nothing but superior ratings in all my work evaluations until this guy was promoted."

"Was he a work colleague?" I asked.

"No, he was promoted from another office."

"Well, that may explain some of it!" I said.

"It doesn't explain it to me."

"You are a threat to him. You know the job better than he does."

"True, and he knows it."

I suggested that Larry stop taking solutions to his boss. I explained, "That just shows him you know the answers and he doesn't. He might think you are after his job."

Remember that the Affect Gauge and Affect Generation and Conservation Charts include a list for generating positive affect and a separate list for conserving the energy generated. One of the things on the list is the reduction of nonproductive behaviors, such as gaming behaviors. In Larry's case, I worked with him to help him recognize his boss's gaming behaviors and explained the Rescue Triangle to him. The Rescue Triangle, a psychological and social model of human interaction in transactional analysis (TA), was first described by Dr. Steve Karpman in 1968 as the Karpman Drama Triangle (Karpman, 1968, pp. 39–43).

Here's how the Rescue Triangle works. Many people are locked into an interaction in which they are Rescuer, Persecutor, or Victim. Try to remember someone you know who is forever "helping" someone needy. That's the role of Rescuer. In some instances, the person needing help goes right on needing help and demanding more of the Rescuer until the Rescuer is exhausted. Still, the demands continue. The Rescuer has now become a Victim. Rescuers-turned-Victim become resentful, but go on helping anyway. They begin to feel that they are being used, and then become Persecutors, striking out at the Victim. Most typically, the Rescuer-turned-Persecutor can't resist rescuing someone else, and the Triangle repeats itself.

A clear example of this Triangle is seen in domestic violence cases. During home calls, police arresting the abusing partner are sometimes attacked by the victimized partner. In a 2009 article in *The American*

Journal of Family Therapy, Luciano L'Abate suggested that the Drama Triangle, with its Victim, Persecutor, and Rescuer roles, originated in 1968 by S. B. Karpman, hadn't received due attention from the family therapy profession, even though it was evident where emotional, sexual and physical abuse were present.

I helped Larry see that he was playing the Rescuer by taking solutions to his new boss. His boss, instead of being grateful, was threatened by Larry's knowledge and became angry. He was on the lookout for ways to criticize Larry and his work. Larry's boss had become a Persecutor. Larry, who thought he was helping by being a Rescuer, was now a Victim.

When Larry understood what had been happening, he no longer took solutions to his boss and the initial trigger for the Rescue Triangle was eliminated. Once Larry broke out of the Rescue Triangle, he and his boss developed a testy but workable relationship. By filling and conserving his affect tank, Larry was better able to cope on the job.

With these three clients, I was able to apply the principles of engineering to psychotherapy. I was able to help Joyce discover the many resources she had in her affect tank, to socialize more, and quell her loneliness. Lee's program of constructive worrying helped him move his affect from negative to positive. For Larry, eliminating the stress that his "helpful" behavior caused and avoiding the Rescue Triangle provided greater stores of resiliency. For all three clients, their emotions became well-calibrated and their affect tanks full, and I was able to teach them to manage their affect reserves for a lifetime of happiness and fulfillment.

7 The Psychotherapist as Master Chef

I was recently reading *Notes on Cooking: A Short Guide to an Essential Craft* (Costello & Reich, 2009). This primer is made up of some 217 tips to help anyone improve their cooking. Several of their cooking tips easily apply to psychotherapy—and can be useful therapeutic metaphors to help clients change their behavior and their emotions. Here are some examples that resonated with me:

Work from your strengths.
Aim at mastery of craft, not of art.
Above all, do no harm.
Please, please, slow down.
Preside happily over accidents.
Hand-select your ingredients.

It goes without saying that the master chef is the leader of a team that might include everyone from the suppliers to the pastry chef, line cook, *sous* chef, and sommelier. But it is the master chef who is responsible for making certain that the ingredients, timing, heat, and presentation come together into an exquisite meal.

So it is with the psychotherapist, who is selecting a mode of treatment based on his knowledge of client behavior. He or she is aware of the client dynamics and is sensitive to timing, pressure, and presentation. Like the preparation of a meal, psychotherapy is a process where all these things come together for the good of the client.

I remember going to the famed New Orleans restaurant Antoine's with a friend, Roy, who had developed a very sophisticated palate. We were both barely 21, and had just finished Officers' Training at Fort Benning, Georgia. En route to report to Fort Ord, California, my culinarily experienced friend wanted to introduce me to French cooking, and where better to start than one of the most famous French restaurants in the country? I anticipated the meal with both apprehension and curiosity.

Roy had been raised in New York and Paris, and he began the meal, speaking in French, by reviewing the wine list with the sommelier and then the menu with the waiter. He explained to me that he had ordered a special meal with wines to complement each course. Unlike many first-time gourmet diners, I had the company of a well-versed connoisseur. As we ate, Roy explained the origin of ingredients, the preparation, and the cooking for each dish. He brought the efforts of the master chef and the machinations of the restaurant kitchen to life for me.

The waiter brought every course in anticipation of our pleasure. He presented each dish with flair. He knew that what he was presenting was an exquisite meal, and my friend, with his French gusto for food, praised every dish. It was a culinary delight and a powerful learning experience for me. At the end of the meal, Roy went to the kitchen to compliment the master chef. I tagged along, learning as I went.

Afterwards, Roy explained to me that the preparation of food, by most passionate chefs, is done with great care and attention to detail. It's both an art and a science, and the chef always has in mind his diners' reactions. Jonah Lehrer, in his book *Proust was a Neuroscientist* (2007), makes a distinct point about the art and science of cooking in his discussion of Auguste Escoffier. In a chapter aptly titled "The Essence of Taste," we learn how the great French chef discovered "umami," known as the fifth taste. Popularly referred to as savoriness, it is considered one of the five basic tastes, along with sweet, sour, bitter, and salt. Escoffier believed that every dish should be cooked perfectly, using the best ingredients, the most careful cooking, and the most attractive presentation. And of course the timing has to be perfect.

This nurturing concern mirrors that of the psychotherapist. Like the master chef, the psychotherapist's success is contingent on exceeding the diner's or client's expectations. For both the master chef and the psychotherapist, part of the preparation is creating reasonable and positive expectations. Like the psychotherapist, the master chef in a fine restaurant is always thinking ahead. But, as you will see, not even the wisest or most experienced chef or psychotherapist can anticipate fully how the diner, or client, will react to the experience.

What is the first thing good chefs do? They rise early to get to the market and purchase the freshest, most succulent vegetables and fruit. They check their supplies of staples. They order meat, fish, and cheese from reliable sources. Based on what's available, they plan a menu.

A good example of choosing ingredients in psychotherapy comes from selecting individuals for group therapy. Just as the chef's menu features a diversity of ingredients, colors, and textures, well-functioning therapy groups contain a mix of life experiences, complexity of problems, and client interactions. These ingredients dictate if and how the group comes together cohesively. I have worked with groups, as I'm sure many of my colleagues have done, in which all the participants had similar problems and similar levels of distress. These groups can become monotonous, just as meals that consist of just one texture, taste, or color are monotonous.

I believe that variety is an important ingredient in effective groups, just as it is in a great gustatory experience.

Case 27: Mabel Ann and Bill

My wife and I led a couples' group in which one of the husbands was the minister of a small country church. Reverend Bill was a short, energetic, big-voiced, nervous man with an opinion about almost everything. His wife, Mabel Ann, appeared to be a nearly perfect pastor's wife as the leader of many church activities, a member of the choir, a greeter, and a book club participant. She provided food for funerals and participated in community outreach. She did it all with grace and cheer.

Reverend Bill and Mabel Ann were quiet during the early sessions of group therapy, reluctant to talk about their problems and, as they admitted later, apprehensive about even admitting that they had any kind of marital difficulty. They were there because they had heard of the successes of previous groups, some of which included members of their congregation. They felt that learning more about our groups would benefit their ministry. I suspected their interest went beyond mild curiosity, but while I had misgivings, I encouraged them to come. Once they had attended a few sessions, it became apparent they were concerned that word of their seeking help might get back to their congregation and that there might be repercussions. They worried that any disclosure, even in the privacy of the group, could cost Reverend Bill his church. Consequently, they were pretty reserved during the early sessions.

Despite their reserve, however, they were willing to do their part in a number of ways. For instance, early in the establishment of the group, the members decided they wanted refreshments after the meetings, and, not surprisingly, Mabel Ann was quick to volunteer. She brought enough fresh cupcakes and delicious herbal tea for at least 30 people. There were five couples in the group.

Mabel Ann was always ready to support and comfort any of the women who became upset by what was revealed in the group. At the same time, many of the group members were already disturbed by Reverend Bill's overintellectualized problem solving.

About 3 months after the group began, one of the women took Bill to task for his unfeeling response to her anguish about her discovery that her husband had had an affair. Then another woman accused Bill of having no real feelings for people in pain. Mabel Ann suddenly jumped up and screamed that Bill had struck her repeatedly; she accused him of being a wife-beater and having "no empathy for anyone." She told the group that she hated Bill and was going to leave him. Then she ran out of the room, sobbing uncontrollably.

I asked my wife to help the group process what had just happened, and I went to find Mabel Ann, wondering just what I was going to say.

I knew, much like a master chef facing a culinary disaster, that when the pot boils over, it doesn't have to ruin the entire meal. In fact, it can create the spark for new things to happen. As Costello and Reich (2009) reminded their readers, "Preside happily over accidents." And they also cautioned, "Get the habit of celebrating errors and seeking lessons."

That is exactly what we did in the group. We let things cool down a bit and then processed what Mabel Ann, Bill, and the rest of the group made of the situation. Often therapeutic progress is the direct result of outbursts like this.

When I caught up with Mabel Ann, she was really grateful that I had come after her. She immediately remembered that when she was growing up and became upset, she was ignored, which always made her feel abandoned. She said, "If I show my real feelings, no one will love me." For some reason, I was immediately reminded of my wonderful mother-in-law's mantra about gravy-making: "Never let the gravy get the upper hand! When the flour and grease are all stuck in the center of the pan, just add the liquid and stir and stir, until something good happens."

So I stirred. I talked to Mabel Ann for nearly an hour about Bill.

She explained to me, "He is a perfectionist. He loses his temper, and sometimes he hits me."

She continued, "It hurts, but not nearly as much as being discounted as I was by my family." So she had tolerated Bill's abuse.

Between sobs, Mabel Ann said, "I am so glad that I told the group about this." I reminded her that domestic violence, regardless of provocation, is never excusable, and emphasized that she was not responsible for the violence on the occasions when she "didn't get it right." I asked her to place the blame where it belonged.

Mabel Ann had been afraid that if the group learned the truth about her and the Reverend, they would reject them both. I reassured her that the group had concerns of their own to worry about. I suggested that she would really be doing the group a great service by coming back and talking about the abuse and asking for the group's help. Like a master chef, I knew what the ingredients were for this group's therapeutic activation. I knew that groups often have a remarkable resilience and can respond in the most wonderful and supportive ways.

Mabel Ann cautiously came back to the group, sitting a fair distance away from her husband. When I asked the group to fill us in on their discussion during our absence, they told us that Bill had shamefacedly admitted losing his temper and shoving her on a number of occasions, screaming at her that she "couldn't do anything right." In Mabel Ann's presence, the group insisted on a sworn pledge from Bill on the Bible that he would never commit such an outrage again. He even went out to his car to get his own Bible. The group welcomed Mabel Ann back and reiterated their own commitment to make sure the pledge was honored and that the discovery would never go beyond the confines of the group. Mabel Ann was reassured on both counts.

The ingredient mix of the group led to some interesting dynamics. The women continued to be very sensitive to the possibility of domestic violence of every variety: physical, verbal, and emotional. They checked with each other at almost every session to make sure that no one had been threatened or hurt. They were a sisterhood in this regard.

Interestingly, Reverend Bill became somewhat more subdued and far less prone to intellectualize. His reputation as a know-it-all had been remarkably reduced. He was not always liked, but was now more roundly accepted as a member of the group.

When you have good ingredients, a good outcome can usually be expected. In this case, the addition of considerable heat was just what the group needed to be cohesive. I was concerned that perhaps Mabel Ann's explosion had generated too much heat. But it became clear that this incident had been exactly what was needed to motivate this group to work together.

The group continued for another 6 months. Except for one couple, everyone reported that the group experience had strengthened their marriage. The one exception, Ruth and Greg, decided to divorce, but they felt that this decision was positive, ending a silent, angry truce in which they had engaged for many years. Other people may have considered Ruth and Greg's marriage a failure—like a dessert that's flipped over by mistake. But the group helped them come to a clear decision and both were comfortable with the outcome.

Case 28: Ruth and Greg

Ruth and Greg had come into the group with very much their own agenda. Ruth had stated during the initial screening evaluation, which I always used before beginning a group, that she knew that the marriage was a mistake even before the wedding. "It was one of those things that had its own momentum. There was just no good place to stop. After we had sex and I told him we should get married, he agreed, and so we did. That's part of the problem; he just goes along with whatever I tell him to do."

Greg was subdued during his initial screening. His story matched what Ruth had told me. He said, "I grew up with an absent father, a powerful 11th-grade math teacher as a mother, and two older, smarter sisters. The safest thing for me to do was to just go along. They were in charge of my life from day one. They told me when to get up, when to go to bed, and everything in between. My reward was that I didn't have to do anything. Beth, my older sister, even did most of my homework for me."

He continued, "Ruth and I started dating as seniors in high school. After graduation, she announced that we were going to be married, and the rest is history. Now that I think back, I realize that she has never really liked me, and now she wants to divorce me. It's not fair."

In the group, the women almost immediately rallied around Ruth, feeling that Greg was a passive simpleton. The men were at first defensive about him and then they decided that the women were ganging up on him. They launched a program to give him some backbone. During the subsequent sessions Greg seemed to grow in confidence and began speaking up, first to help others and then to help himself.

During the last few weeks of the group, Greg challenged Ruth and told her, in the group's presence, that he was sick and tired of being her garbage can and that he wanted out. The men in the group quietly cheered. Ruth was stunned, almost feeling as if she had made a mistake in trying to get rid of him. But her long history of contempt for his passivity prevailed and she decided that one-more-chance would be foolish. She agreed to the divorce. The group supported them. Shortly after that, they were divorced.

The group had a potluck supper at the end of the final session. Everyone brought a delicious dish. For me, this potluck became a metaphor for the kinds of sharing the group had done. The members had talked about their worries, fears, and solutions, and now they had a great meal, celebrating their collective success.

This therapy experience provided me with a real opportunity to work with a very diverse group. I had frankly been reluctant to admit ministers into a therapy group. It had been my experience that members of the group tended to defer to them, interfering with the group process. I had also tended to run groups in which everyone was fairly well educated. This group's education ranged from master's degrees to high school dropouts. The variety of experience, education, and background proved to be useful. My personal belief that diversity lends itself to the effectiveness of groups is supported by James Simpkin, the author of "Gestalt Therapy in Groups." In this article, he says about the formulation of groups, "Attempts were made to insure the heterogeneity of the groups by bringing in a wide range of age, occupation, presenting problems, etc. as was possible from the sources available ..." (Simkin, 1975, p. 276). I'm reminded once again of the qualities of a good chef, who strives for diversity in tastes and textures.

Chefs also like to use a variety of tools. Most carry their own collection of knives with them. Well-known chef Tom Coliccio, in his book *Think Like a Chef* (2000), talks about a knife he has had since he was 15. He relates a story of a knife he received for Christmas when he was 15, which he still uses. Many chefs like the experience of visiting other kitchens to see other chefs in action. They are excited to learn new approaches and techniques, and to observe different ways to ply the tools of their trade. As a psychotherapist, I have experienced that excitement when learning about other professionals' work. I once attended a workshop based on two of Martin Seligman's books, *Learned Optimism* (1998) and *Authentic Happiness* (2002) that gave me a new way to work with clients. I returned to my practice excited and renewed.

There is a lot of science, especially chemistry, involved in food preparation. Think about the different ways that a chef can apply heat: toast, roast, boil, grill, braise, sear, broil, bake, steam, sauté, poach, and simmer, each of which creates different results. The braised beef is tender and succulent; the grilled chicken holds its juice and has a beautiful crispy skin. A seared tenderloin reveals its rare flavor when the knife cuts into it. The gently simmered risotto yields the flavors of the broth, wine, butter, and mushrooms within it.

So it is in psychotherapy. Let's go back to our couples' group. There were participants like Bill and Mabel Ann, who spent their first sessions with the group on a slow simmer, watching carefully and guardedly and keeping tight control of the temperature of their encounter with the others. When Bill and Mabel Ann's pot boiled over, their relationship reached a point of crisis, and the group was able to help them deal with it. Others in the group were more vocal, or more impulsive, wanting to toss their resentments on a hot grill and sear the daylights out of their partners. Sometimes it worked, and sometimes it didn't. But my job in this kitchen of group dynamics was to temper the heat, not necessarily take things off the fire entirely, but assure that no one got too overwhelmed or underwhelmed. There can be too little as well as too much heat, after all.

Case 29: Janey and Her Family

One of the key talents of the psychotherapist who functions as a master chef is to know how to time the use of heat to produce the best results. This is especially true in family therapy, where a psychotherapist may have many things cooking at the same time. In the following case, I actually applied almost overwhelming heat to the mother, father, and son. At the same time, I was guarding the daughter, who was the victim, by protecting her from the heat.

I spoke by phone with the mother, Janine. Her daughter, Janey, had told her pediatrician that she had been sexually molested by her older half-brother, Joey. The pediatrician, an older, wise, gentle woman, suggested that Janine and her family see me. When I asked Janine what expectations she had of family therapy, she said, "I want you to get my daughter to quit saying such horrible things about my son." I was shocked at Janine's expectation, but I agreed to see the family. I knew this pediatrician and respected her judgment. First I saw 13-year-old Janey, who was both subdued and anxious. She also seemed very fearful.

She said to me, "I don't want to do this. Joey will kill me if he thinks I've told on him."

Later in this family's treatment, I learned that he had indeed threatened her. I reassured her that, although her parents were skeptical, I believed her when she told me she had been sexually molested. She was reassured by this. I also reassured her that I would find ways to protect her, and I told her that for starters, Joey would not be living in the same house. She was very grateful. She waited in another room with a female colleague of mine. I didn't want her to have to see her brother, who I interviewed next.

Joey was a husky 17-year-old who appeared confident, almost arrogant.

"Hey, I didn't do *anything*. This is just Janey being crazy and making stuff up."

He continued to deny the abuse for quite awhile. I was finally able to silence him by bringing up the investigation that was in progress.

"So," I said carefully, "if this is all about nothing, why do you think that Family Services are investigating?"

This question was received with a sullen silence. I closed the interview and told him I would see him the following week.

His mother and father were next. Janine was angry and upset with Janey and defensive about Joey, with whom she had had a good relationship:

"He could not possibly have done anything sexual to his little sister," she told me. Her husband, Ted, was a quiet, tense man, big and broad-shouldered. He appeared detached and puzzled. It was apparent that he had not been aware of the abuse or any of its signs.

As his wife talked about the case, he became angrier and angrier. I decided not to confront him. I listened quietly.

"This is nonsense. This is nothing but Janine being hysterical. And that stupid doctor...." As his voice trailed off, he reddened and shook his fist. He wanted to call a halt to the therapy. The first thing I did was remind the two of them that the case was already under investigation, and recommend that Joey move out of the house immediately as part of the effort to protect Janey. I also emphasized that Janey's only contact with Joey should be in the safe environment of our therapy sessions. Ted became even angrier. Sexual abuse cases are not for the faint of heart.

The sessions that followed included meetings with Joey and his step-parents, and sessions alone with Janey. Janine expressed anger at Janey: "Why is she making up these lies and causing all this trouble for our family?" Ted continued to be angry and incredulous: "How could this have happened without me knowing anything about it?" he asked. Joey was guileless, continuing to deny that anything had happened.

During her sessions alone, Janey was furious with her brother. "He's wrecked everything for me. It's his entire fault." She viewed herself as being a "troublemaker."

The heat was high in the sessions I conducted with the parents and the brother. By our third session, we reached a critical point in therapy. I would compare the process of escalating heat to that of a chef making chicken soup. When the chef immerses the whole chicken in water with onion, carrots and soup greens, the surface of the water should have what chefs call a "smile," that is, it barely ripples. But beneath the surface, the heat of the stove is doing its work. Coaxing the flavor from the vegetables as they gently cook with the chicken into a rich broth may be the most critical step in making chicken soup and a key to its curative powers.

So it was with this family. As we sorted through the suspicions, anger, and blame, the heat was on. Janine now painfully acknowledged her son's sexual predation. The heat was turned up further when Janine learned that two of Janey's friends had been sexually abused by Joey. There was also a report filed against Joey for date rape. At the same time, Janey's case, which was being investigated by Family Services, was about to be turned over to the State's Attorney as a criminal case.

Janine now realized that by not believing that her daughter had been molested, she had further victimized her. She felt guilty about Janey and betrayed by Joey. She was also furious with herself. Ted was numb and still disengaged. During this time it became evident that Ted had been drinking a lot over the past few years, which may have explained his lack of awareness about what was going on. Joey continued to insist that he had done nothing and that Janey was making the story up because she was jealous of him. For Janey, her parents' acknowledgment that she was the telling the truth was a relief.

Because the case had now reached a point of high heat, I used components from a 16-step method that was specifically created to treat families involved with sexual abuse. The methods had been developed by one of family therapy's master teachers, Cloe Madanes, author of *Sex, Love, and Violence: Strategies for Transformation* (1990). I had been a trainee at her Family Therapy Institute. In the program, which she ran with Jay Haley, I had seen her apply some the techniques she described in her book. I selected three of them.

The first step was to put the heat on Joey. In Madanes's words, this step is "to obtain an account of the sexual offense ..." (Madanes, 1990, p. 52). I confronted Joey in his parents' presence until I had that account, and Joey had admitted, "Yeah, well, maybe I did fool around with her a little." The second step was to ask Joey to apologize, on his knees, to his sister. Madanes suggests that the therapist "ask the offender to get on his knees in front of the victim and express sorrow and repentance for what he did" (Madanes, 1990, p. 53). During one session, with Janey safely in another room, I repeatedly asked Joey to beg Janey's forgiveness on his knees. He was adamant in his refusal. I stopped the session, telling Janine and Ted, "We absolutely cannot go on until Joey is willing to admit to the molestation in front of Janey and to apologize." I also reminded them that as a mandated reporter, I could be asked under oath whether Joey showed remorse, and that my answer would be a distinct "no." They begged Joey to apologize, actually getting on *their* hands and knees. He refused.

When the three of them came in the following week, I spent the first half hour of the session again persuading Joey to apologize. Finally, Joey reluctantly got out of his chair and crept forward on his hands and knees. His voice barely audible, he whispered, "I'm sorry."

I brought Janey into the room. It was the first time she had seen him since he had left the home. With her mother and father on either side, she sat in front of her brother, her parents' arms around her. Joey again mumbled, "I'm sorry." I had him repeat it and add the promise that he would do anything he could in the years to come to help Janey make a good life for herself. He mumbled this, too. The second step had been taken, and the session was over.

At the next session I applied a third step from Madanes's book: finding ways for the family, including Joey, to commit fully to Janey's emotional support. This support extended far beyond a pledge that the family acknowledge the harm done. They had to affirm their commitment to do everything in their power to assure that Janey was protected and aided in rebuilding her self-esteem, sexual boundaries, and her entire life.

Madanes speaks of another step—"reparation"—that I would have liked to apply in this case. Reparation means that the victim's parents are asked to "think about what the offender could do as an act of reparation" (Madanes, 1990, p. 55). Madanes acknowledges that usually "the reparation is somewhat symbolic because there is really nothing he can do to compensate for sexual violence" (Madanes, 1990, p. 55). This was certainly true in Joey's case.

After another 12 sessions, the family, except for Joey, who had been sent to a juvenile correctional facility, was able to spend meaningful time together. Ted had found sobriety after years of drinking, and Janine renewed friendships she had lost. Some new ingredients had brought them closer together: forgiveness on Janey's part and Janine's recognition of her misplaced loyalty to Joey and her refusal to believe Janey were replaced with a new love and appreciation for her daughter. Their efforts continued as they restructured their family. I felt I had been a reasonably good chef, helping this family weather the heat of the kitchen.

I stayed in touch with the family for many years. Janey married and had a child. Joey disappeared, violating his probation. Janine told me that they were grateful for the part I'd played in the healing process. Madanes (1990) emphasizes that:

In cases of incest and sexual abuse there are several important principles to remember:

1. The therapist must emphasize that the sexual offense was a violation of the spirit of the victim.
2. The offender must express repentance sincerely and on his knees.
3. Reparation must take place.
4. All secrets must be violated.

For this family, I wanted first to rescue and protect Janey. My second objective was to save the family. Both efforts were successful, although Joey was no longer a member of the family. I do wonder, though, if I could have done more to help him.

When operating as a master chef, the psychotherapist has to be an expert at using heat, but he or she also needs to use exquisitely good timing. The length of cooking—how long to simmer, boil, bake, or fry—makes an enormous difference in the finished product. Even more important, the components of the entire dining experience—food cooked and prepared in different ways, sometimes by different chefs—must all come together on the table.

When we go to a fine restaurant most of the preparation of our order is invisible. It comes to us hot, with wonderful tastes and aromas, and often beautiful to behold. Although some chefs strive to make the preparation of a dish look effortless, it's always a complex process.

The same can be said of psychotherapy. Those not involved in the process might see it as a simple set of conversations that take place over a period of time. But looking back at cases like that of Janey and her family, I wonder what would have happened if I had pushed harder for Joey to beg forgiveness. If I had pushed him too hard, he might have continued to resist. If I had delayed, Janey's critical need for family support might never have been met. Though I was unsure at the time whether I was applying the right amount of psychological heat, the positive outcomes of the case tell me I did the right thing.

Case 30: Terry

In the planning and cooking of a fine meal, there is a final component to be considered: presentation. I've already described the beautiful plates set in front of me at Antoine's, as well as the quiet attentiveness of the waiter and the pride of the wait staff as they presented each course to my dining companion and me. Their positive expectation of our pleasure was real and contagious.

I thought about presentation when I saw a client, Terry, a big, good-looking, athletic 34-year-old. His employer, a dynamic technology firm, had asked him to take a personality inventory, the 16PF, before they considered him for a new overseas position with major responsibilities. The test measures 16 personality traits and gives some indication of potential job performance.

Terry was worried about what the 16PF would say about him. He was afraid the findings would go on his record and disqualify him for the job or for other jobs in the future. In talking with him, I didn't get the sense that he was hiding anything; rather that he was self-conscious and insecure. In order to get this job, which he wanted very badly, the test was required, so he was eager to take it, but very worried about its findings.

I was concerned that his high level of anxiety could affect test results, so I prepared him for the test by giving him considerably more reassurance than I would have routinely. I explained to him that the results could not be made available to anyone but his employer. I also emphasized that in my professional opinion, having seen him for several hours, that he was emotionally well-adjusted, had some considerable psychological strengths, and wasn't going to find out anything he didn't already know about himself. This was my way of prepping him for the test and its results. He was still anxious and insecure.

When Terry's test results came in, all the scales were in the normal range, with some lower scores in areas like self-confidence and self-esteem. He was relieved, and I was not surprised. I then used the test results to point out his psychological strength. I applauded him for his open, truthful responses on the test and helped him use the information the test provided.

This case demonstrated to me the need for careful presentation. Had Terry's test anxiety increased, it might have been reflected in the test. Presenting the test to him as a tool to identify his own psychological strengths became a way of reassuring Terry rather than threatening his career possibilities. (Terry did, by the way, get the overseas position he had wanted.)

In this chapter, I have examined four key components that apply both to the practices of the master chef and to the psychotherapist applying culinary principles: ingredients, heat, timing, and presentation. For the diner, the correct mix of these elements assures a pleasurable experience. In psychotherapy, incorporating these components into treatment will expand the practice of the psychotherapist and improve the outcomes for the client.

8 The Psychotherapist as Music Teacher

I took piano lessons for 5 years when I was young. I didn't realize until much later what an amazingly sensitive and accepting teacher I had. Looking back, I recognize that what I learned (besides how to play the piano rather poorly) was behavior I saw my teacher Mrs. Cox model: patience, warmth, flexibility, tact, understanding, and wisdom in setting and achieving goals. Shouldn't these same qualities apply to the effective psychotherapist?

I remember reporting for my weekly lesson, thoroughly unpracticed. Mrs. Cox explored the problem, which stemmed in part from the teasing I was getting from my friends. When they asked what tunes I was learning to play and I told them Mozart and Debussy, they fell on the ground laughing. With surprising empathy, Mrs. Cox started adapting popular songs for me to practice and learn. I still had to go through John Thompson's *Modern Course for the Piano* (1937), but at the start of many lessons she would play a piece of popular music that she had simplified for me to learn. While I didn't thoroughly appreciate it at the time, I hereby send her a much belated thanks. Besides finding a way to maintain my motivation, she modeled a wonderful understanding of human behavior.

Part of what Mrs. Cox taught me was how to listen, which, of course, turns out to be an invaluable skill for psychotherapists to master. We grow up thinking we know how to listen, when in fact, listening takes attentive awareness. Studying music can teach us to practice active listening. We become more aware of pitch, volume, rhythm, harmony, melody, brightness, tempo, and dissonance, among other things. What Mrs. Cox used to tell me was not just to play the notes, but to tell a musical story that people could hear and understand. I believe that most of us have to practice this kind of awareness to be able to listen well. This is what those years of piano lessons taught me. While I didn't become an accomplished pianist, I did learn how to listen. This led to an approach to treating clients in a way I think of as the psychotherapist as music teacher.

Something else happened during those 5 years of lessons: recitals—one of the most painful experiences I have ever had to endure. I hated them and begged to be excused, but to no avail. Before and during every recital I was certain that I would make gruesome mistakes. And my performance panic never let up. I suspect that these recitals were probably painful for Mrs. Cox, too. Why didn't she just forget about them? As I look back, I realize she kept up the tradition of recitals because they served a valuable purpose for me and her other students. Preparing for a recital required me to set goals and work with a timetable. Setting goals against a deadline is a powerful formula for changing behavior; it requires hard practice on a regular basis.

Case 31: Eleanor

With this understanding of the music teacher's role, let me offer an example of this model in action in psychotherapy. For a time, I had a client who had been seriously injured in an automobile accident. Eleanor was on antidepressants 2 months after the accident. She was still very tense and anxious and she was suffering from nightmares. Getting into her car was almost impossible. By the time she came to my office, she was gray and visibly shaking.

She described the pain she was in from spinal fractures incurred in the accident. She also told me about her nightmares and anxiety. She was going about her normal activities, she said, and had not discussed how she felt, until now, with anyone but her doctor.

She said her current physical and emotional state "was desperate." I asked her if she could tell me about the accident.

"I was driving home from choir practice. I wasn't joy-riding or speeding or anything, and then the crash. I was in the hospital for 2½ weeks. Now it's been 3 months and I'm still in considerable pain and fear. I can hardly drive."

I invited her to talk about her life before she was injured. I wanted to move her attention away from her current situation and to learn more about her. She described her life before the accident as being almost idyllic. She and her two younger brothers had grown up in a small farm town close to her grandparents, who owned and operated a successful farm supply store.

She had experienced very little adversity. Grade school, high school, and 2 years of college were happy and unremarkable. She had been married for 4 years and described her marriage as happy. Had I expressed Eleanor's past life in musical terms, it would have been a nice little tune, somewhat repetitive, in a major key. Her current emotional state in musical terms would have been a repetitive and off-key minor melody.

My job as a psychotherapist adapting the role of music teacher was to be patient, listen to the music of Eleanor's experience, and urge her to move past the painful and repetitive notes so that she might find some relief from the anxiety and pain that was plaguing her. As she was not able to identify any really tough times in her own life, I asked her to talk to her mother and grandmother about tough times the family might have gone through. I thought this would be a way for her to discover how her family, which she was close to, had coped with hardship.

After she talked to her mother and grandmother, Eleanor told me about her grandfather, who had come home from World War II withdrawn, tense, and nervous. He never talked about his war experiences, but when he returned to a business and a community that had been changed by the war, his approach was, "We will work our way through this." Eleanor's grandmother told her, "There's no point in dwelling on bad things."

"Don't dwell on the bad" seemed to be a family motto. In family lore, Eleanor's grandfather used to dispense this advice to customers who came into his store with a sad story about a broken plow or a failed crop. He was something of a natural problem-solver for farm problems; he always remembered the year that there was no rain and everyone in the community hunkered down for a devastating time. The business had drastically shrunk. But all he would say was, "We will work our way through this."

I suggested that Eleanor ask her grandmother to tell her more about the near-collapse of the family business. I hoped that this would give her an example of overcoming adversity. "Ask your grandmother what happened when the family business was about to collapse."

Several weeks later, Eleanor told me the story her grandmother had told her. It seemed that the family, in the face of adversity, sang "I've been working on the railroad" over and over again. I suggested to Eleanor that she join the family chorus.

The "we will work through this" approach was something Eleanor understood. I decided to use our time together to help her use this approach in her current situation. I knew from my piano recital experience that if you expect to hit bad notes, you will. Eleanor expected to be in pain, and since her accident, she had not been disappointed.

I began by giving her a practice assignment. I asked her to think about good and bad things that had happened to her and her family and to make a note of them. Keeping the list, she began recognizing her family's resiliency in the face of negative events. She asked me, "How can I get better at being resilient?" and I answered, "How do you get better at anything? Practice, practice, practice." I drew an analogy to my early piano lessons. "My piano teacher urged me to practice," I explained. "She wanted at least an hour a day."

One of the ways Eleanor and I practiced was by using imagery and systematic desensitization. I had her visualize getting into and out of her car, and I taught her relaxation procedures that she could practice before and during driving. She became impatient with the effort of doing the relaxation exercises every time she wanted to go someplace, but I told her the story of Nadia Boulanger, one of the most famous music teachers of all time. In *Mademoiselle: Conversations with Nadia Boulanger* (Montsaingeon, 1985), Boulanger is quoted as saying, "I require [my pupils] every week to play a prelude and fugue by heart." The interviewer objected, saying, "But those are draconian demands!" She replied, "Draconian, nonsense. They are needed to help develop musical memory!" (p. 43).

I told Eleanor, "If you want to achieve a new outlook, you have to practice much, much more. Perseverance in your practice and confidence in your abilities are the building blocks of resilience." It may be unrealistic for psychotherapists to expect clients to change their behavior with an hour of psychotherapy a week, rather than suggesting, like a demanding music teacher, several hours of faithful practice a day. Doesn't the degree of improvement in any developed skill correspond to the amount of time invested? That's why I encouraged Eleanor to practice resiliency outside our sessions. As we worked together, Eleanor continued to express the desire to become more resilient, hopeful, and optimistic. Once she resolved to work hard and long at her recovery, we started to make significant progress. Eleanor and I set a goal that required measurable progress within a defined time period, as a way to encourage more practice and build Eleanor's confidence in her driving ability. After a year, her pain and fear had dissipated. Her practice had resulted in a more positive, more optimistic, and resilient Eleanor. I suspect that is just what Mrs. Cox was trying to achieve. (It didn't work for me, because I didn't practice!)

Case 32: Jeff

I became more aware of my ability to function like a music teacher when a sad-looking 50-year-old man, Jeff, came to see me. He had been referred by his physician for depression and anxiety. Several months of taking antidepressant medication had helped, but he was still troubled. We spent most of our first three sessions talking about how discouraged he was about his state of mind, but he couldn't identify anything that had triggered it.

When I run into impasses like this, I usually suggest we go back to before the anxiety set in and do a "life review." I said to Jeff, "Let's look at what you were doing before and around the time the bad feelings set in." He had identified that time as 4 to 6 months earlier.

"Okay, so let's talk about August and September. What was going on?"

"Nothing special, nothing in particular," was his uninformative response.

"So talk for a while about nothing in particular," I said, which made us both smile.

He talked about his wife and two grown kids. One son had a good job and the other was in college. Then he talked a little about his own job. He had been working for the state in a technical position for 11 years and said it was "all right." Nothing there either.

"I like my job. It's neither ugly nor pleasant, usually not particularly exciting or boring." And then the timbre of his voice changed. It got a little rough, so I started listening more carefully.

He went on to tell me about giving a brief report at a staff meeting. The report went well, but afterward one of his colleagues (whom he wasn't particularly fond of) said to him offhandedly, "That wasn't much of a report you gave." His response was, "No, there wasn't much to say."

Jeff went on. "But that remark somehow stuck in my craw. The truth was it wasn't much of a report, but I had never openly criticized his half-ass reports. What gave him the right to criticize mine?"

"But it got me thinking," he continued. "How many of my reports had been slipshod and how often had my colleagues thought less of me for them?" Then he went on to talk about other things in his life, and the timbre of his voice returned to normal.

A session later, we still hadn't found anything in particular, so I asked him to go back and recall that report. He expressed surprised at my request, smiled, and then repeated the story, with more details, but the same rough-timbred sound. When he finished, he smiled wanly and said, "My self-esteem took a hit." I nodded and he shook his head, commenting, "And he's not even a friend of mine. Why should I care?"

"Maybe because, in your mind, he was right, and maybe he wasn't even trying to help," I suggested.

So we focused on his self-esteem as it related to his job. When I asked him about his self-esteem in social situations, he told me his social relationships were generally good to near excellent. He and his wife had a very positive, loving relationship. He got along wonderfully with his kids (you can't say that about lots of us) and he had a wide circle of friends and a busy social life.

In fact, Jeff had a good job and was well-respected by his employer and colleagues, but he had gotten careless, almost indifferent, in his reporting at quarterly staff meetings. Once this was pointed out to him, he realized that he had come off lacking at these meeting. He was angry at himself and aware that his reputation at work, particularly when he delivered reports to colleagues at meetings, was not as good as he would have liked. He didn't know what he could do to correct it.

Since my musical "ear" had alerted me, I decided to stay in that mode and reactivated how I felt after a couple of terrible and terrifying piano recitals. Mrs. Cox's remedy for almost everything was practice, practice, practice, actually to overlearn the music. I pointed out to Jeff that the rude remark and his reaction could be a wake-up call. He needed to practice writing his reports and memorize them before the meeting.

Jeff objected, insisting that all that effort wasn't appropriate or necessary. But I pointed out that he needed to overcorrect his past sloppy reports, and doing so would mean a lot of extra effort. He reluctantly followed my advice for the next three monthly reports. He was starting to feel a little foolish. A week after he delivered the third carefully worked report, his boss called him in and specifically praised his presentation; he followed that up by including it in his performance appraisal, which got Jeff a commendation and a bonus.

Several months later, at our last session, Jeff and I reviewed where he had been emotionally with staff meetings and self-appraisal, where he was now, and what he was going to do in the future. He laughed and assured me, "I'm going to give hard-hitting reports and get off my antidepressants."

My awareness of what my patients were saying and how they were saying it was raised after that, and I began to make an extra effort to listen to the timbre and intensity of my clients' words. I also resolved to use other aspects of music to increase my awareness and to adopt those qualities as tools for psychotherapy. I was surprised by the variety of aspects I discovered, among them the issue of tempo.

The psychotherapist using the principles and approaches of a music teacher can use changes in tempo to the client's advantage. Sometimes, problems pour out of clients like an overwhelming torrent. I've seen a number of bipolar clients who nearly drowned me in their flood of words and feelings. For such clients I usually recommend medication for their immediate relief. Then I set about interpreting their verbal spillings by posing what I call strategic questions. These kinds of questions don't ask for information. Instead, they redirect the clients' frenzied thoughts toward the "what-ifs" of the situation. What if something else was going on? What if you didn't notice thus and such? What if you had misunderstood what so-and-so said?

Case 33: Sandy

One case in which I used a strategic question to redirect a client's understanding of past events is that of Sandy, a 55-year-old woman with a 26-year-old stepdaughter, Melissa.

Sandy began crying almost as soon as she walked into my office. Through her tears, she began telling me about her experience with Melissa. She described in great detail and at hyperspeed, quieting only to blow her nose, the many times that Melissa had rejected and abused her, accusing her of not caring for her, not doing anything for her, and most important, breaking up her parents' marriage. I learned that Sandy had not even met Melissa's father until he had already been divorced for 2 years.

I needed a show-stopper here. I could see that Sandy had been over and over the same territory many times. I wanted to slow down the pace—tempo, if you will—to give Sandy a chance to see the problem in a new light.

When Sandy finally paused to reach for the tissue box, I asked her, very quietly and slowly, whether it was possible that Melissa somehow felt responsible for her mother's leaving. (I might mention that it is not uncommon, in my experience, for little girls to wish their mothers would leave, so they can have their daddies all to themselves.)

This question stopped Sandy cold. She quit crying immediately and was silent for a moment. As I watched her eyelids flutter, I could see that she was reviewing this possibility. Finally, she spoke, slowly and deliberately. Her affect, no longer frenzied, was thoughtful. I realized that my suggestion to her either had a great deal of truth in it or had caught her totally off guard. Whatever she was thinking, a strategic question broke the blame cycle for Sandy by slowing down and redirecting her train of thought.

Over the next few sessions, Sandy quit examining and reexamining her own feelings and redirected her thoughts to Melissa's state of mind. She was able to give up the guilt she had been heaping upon herself. This slower, more thoughtful tempo benefitted Sandy when she was overwhelmed, by making her step back and see the situation in another way.

Case 34: James

High speed and agitated behavior are at one end of the tempo continuum. On the other end are slowness and depression, which are sometimes part of a bipolar cycle. Nearly everyone practicing psychotherapy has had the experience of calling a new client into the office, watching them take 5 minutes to get across the waiting room floor, all the while never taking their eyes, feet, or body out of the emotional black hole they are living in. The tempo of their emotions can be seen in their body language. And when they speak, their notes, in musical terms, are flat.

I give clients in this state of mind a small task. For instance, for the client I am about to describe, James, I suggested he go back and remember something constructive, something he was proud of.

James was a widower, a slight, stooped man who looked 20 years older than his 60 years. He was hardly able to talk, answering me in monosyllables. In fact, I wasn't sure that he understood my questions, so slow were his responses. It took the first session and much of the second to get his story.

James finally was able to tell me, "My second wife died a little over a year ago. My life has been very bleak, empty." He went on to say that he had been married for 10 years to his first wife, a sweet but remote woman who was addicted to sleeping pills and pain medication. After she died of an overdose, he withdrew from what little social contact he had. James had almost no contact with people except for his colleagues at his job. He worked for the state and had no close friends there. He felt that most likely his colleagues had distanced themselves years ago because of his wife's drug use and his inability to help her.

Imagine how surprised James was when a woman who lived in a neighboring condominium showed interest in him, asking about his backyard garden. They soon began dating rather tentatively, and they married 2 years later. For 5½ years, they did everything together. They did a little traveling and she helped him in the garden. They read a few books together and had, at most, three or four active acquaintances.

Then one day on a work assignment in Chicago, James's second wife was killed in a car accident. She had always been a fearful, hesitant driver, so he wasn't entirely surprised. Besides, he had learned to expect misery. He was still holding down his state job, but just barely. His doctor had put him on a moderate dose of antidepressants and tranquilizers, but because of his experience with his first wife, he didn't like taking drugs. That's when he was referred to me.

James's story came out painfully, slowly, and with a nearly overwhelming sense of loss, grief, and guilt. He also added in passing that he had no one to share his grief with. "I have almost no friends, no social life, no hobbies, no activities, no interests," he said mournfully. I was looking into James's black hole and was struck by how dark and empty his life was. I was not sure how to help him. For an instant, I felt almost as hopeless as he did.

I suggested some regular sessions and pursued one of the few things he had shown interest in: gardening. I got a lukewarm response, but it was a response. He told me that he had kept the garden he had grown with his second wife alive, in spite of his apathy. During the next session, I asked him to recollect where and when he had learned the contentment of watching things grow. It turned out that for years his dad had maintained a rose garden. While James thought it was stupid and avoided working in it, he had picked up the basics. He wasn't sure he liked gardening, but it was something to do. I suggested that he plan to spend a little more time in his garden. He said he would, and after that I noticed that his mood improved ever so slightly.

For the next few sessions, he kept telling me that his gardening was a waste of time and that the garden itself was drying up. I suggested more attention and water. After that, he periodically brought in a story of remembering how tickled his dad had been to discover a new rose variety to plant.

Finally, James's garden started to show improvement. One of his colleagues from work came by and they talked. Some months later, he saw some social life developing, and after turning down two invitations to join the garden club, he relented and became a quiet but active member. He was not a ball of fire by any means, but his energy was rising and at times he smiled a bit. Two years after he began therapy we put our sessions on an "as needed" basis. His work was going fine. He even had a couple of friends. "No women friends yet." He smiled when I repeated "yet." He comes to see me occasionally and brings me a report, and sometimes flowers from his garden. He is not in the black hole, not on medication, and doing okay.

This is an example of using the principles of the music teacher to work with clients to boost the tempo of their lives. In James's case, this amounted to practice assignments that helped him pick up the pace of his life and his interactions with others. His tempo increased, and as it did, his mood improved.

Case 35: Michael

Standing between practice and recital is another important element for music students: rehearsal. The most obvious example of a rehearsal in psychotherapy is "Rehearsals for Living," a technique that I used first in an inpatient setting. You will see how it can also apply to the client in private therapy.

I was working at an inpatient addiction center during a special training program. Instead of a standard psychotherapeutic review, we used drama to help with the discharge process. We called the plays "rehearsals for discharge."

One of the patients facing a rehearsal was Michael, a bright 20-year-old college student who had been hospitalized for 3 months because of an addiction to tranquilizers and whatever street drugs he could buy with his ample allowance. He was sent to several different doctors, and finally one morning his dorm mates couldn't wake him up. When he was discharged from the emergency room, his family arranged for him to be admitted to the private institution where I was working.

For several weeks he had been pestering the staff, particularly his therapist, telling them that he was bored and ready to go home. He wasn't even thinking about getting well any more. His therapist felt that he hadn't come close to dealing with his tension or anxiety, but he was convinced he had. He was sure his therapeutic program had hit the wall. The therapeutic team decided to do a rehearsal and was prepared to send him home if he cleared this hurdle.

In some rehearsals, just before a concert, the conductor takes the musicians through the whole concert. In others, the maestro or maestra just works through the difficult passages. In Michael's case, the discharge team (his psychiatrist, his psychotherapist, and the social worker who did the home coordination) decided to start with the "going home" scenario. If he cleared that, they planned to have him move on to the "going back to school" and "being out with some of his old drug-using friends" as the final pieces for his rehearsal.

They asked Michael to describe his home. They had staff members play his mother, father, and a bright, successful older sister. They gave him a suitcase and had the social worker drop him off at his pretend front door. The family was at the front door waiting for him.

Michael got out of the imaginary car and started up the walk. It was cold in the room but you could see him start to sweat. He waved hesitantly at his mom, who frowned and moved back. His progress up the walk got slower and slower. For him it was a very long walk. About halfway up he stopped, yelled at his mom that he had forgotten something and, dropping his suitcase, ran back to the car. He whispered to the social worker, "I know I'm ready for discharge but I think I'm going to have to have a 'pop' if I have to deal with my mother."

Michael's "rehearsal for discharge" demonstrated to him that he wasn't as ready as he thought. He resumed his work at the center and finally started acknowledging his acute fear of his mom, his resentment of his "spineless" father, and his feelings about his big bad sister.

Two and a half months later another "rehearsal for discharge" showed that Michael was still apprehensive about his mother, but that he could handle those feelings. He also did well in the other parts of the rehearsal and went back to his life. Several months later he told his psychotherapist that the first "rehearsal for discharge" shocked him into working on his problems. His recovery followed.

Two other important aspects of teaching music that the psychotherapist needs to address are timing and blending. I've seen instances when the right thing to say falls on deaf ears. The timing wasn't right. Clients have said that several people had told them what they needed to do, but they just weren't ready to hear it or do it. Effective psychotherapists are acutely aware of when the client is ready to hear and use their observations and suggestions. That's timing. I've heard string quartets in which the cello came in a fraction of a second late. It's jarring and distracting. Good music teachers can help students become more mindful of the flow of the music and to come in more seamlessly. Psychotherapists have the same opportunity to use timing.

There is another therapy technique that I consider musical: blending. Haven't you heard a duet in which two singers actually sing in different keys or notes but sound like one voice because they blend together so beautifully? The psychotherapist, too, can blend his voice with the client's speech as if the two of them shared a voice. This makes it easier for the client to hear and accept the suggestions and ideas that the psychotherapist is raising.

Discordance, another musical term, also plays a part in psychotherapy. Sometimes I need to jar clients to encourage them to abandon a story that is no longer serving its purpose. These no-longer-useful stories are like pieces of music that clients have played over and over and can no longer help them reach their goals. In such cases, like a music teacher, I provide the client with a new piece of music to practice—a new way of looking at their lives. This gives them a chance to perform in different ways. I often disrupt the flow of the client's old story with something that will get their attention, something discordant and shocking.

Case 36: Shari

I once used discord to motivate an attractive 24-year-old client, Shari. She was well-dressed, although somewhat provocatively for the occasion, and had professionally highlighted hair and heavy makeup. From an affluent family, she had been an indifferent student in high school and attended a couple of different colleges for a semester each. Her explanation to me for everything was that she was bored. She attracted plenty of men, but found them boring as well. The friends she had had—and lost—were also defined as boring by her.

Shari clearly needed a new melody. While I rummaged around trying to find some therapeutic "music" that would motivate her, she managed to create her own excitement by getting arrested for shoplifting.

Up until then, she and I had shared some harmonious discussions on her inability to hold onto things she cared about. She liked coming to my office because, as she said, "You're not on my back. You understand." But the session she came in for after the shoplifting incident inspired me to create some disharmony as part of her psychotherapy.

Rather than the blending voice I had used with her previously, I took a more discordant approach. I asked her to relate the experience of her arrest to me. I wanted her to capture in her mind what she was thinking and feeling when she realized that the police were about to arrest her. We went over this experience several times in the next few sessions. She didn't find it comfortable, but with jail time over her head and her parents ready to throw her out, she didn't have much choice.

This incident became the turning point in her therapy. Her discomfort with the discord we had created motivated her to rethink her behavior and its consequences. The jarring experience of being arrested, and then reliving those feelings with me, moved her toward meaningful, positive choices. She realized how often she had thrown away things she cared about and alienated people who cared about her. The cold fact of how close she had come to jail, and my insistence that she relive that experience of her arrest over and over again, motivated her sufficiently that she went back to school to work toward a degree in social justice. This is one of the ways discord can work: as in music, discordant sounds get the audience's attention when they're just about to doze off.

I've only discussed a few aspects of music in this chapter. There are others as well, including beat, rhythm, key, pitch, harmony, and melody.

When psychotherapists apply the concepts of teaching music to their work, they begin to listen to clients discriminately and insist on daily practice as part of the process of change. Does some of this sound off-beat to you?

9 The Psychotherapist as Coach

Virtually everyone who has attended a public high school has had some access to a coach, partly because many coaches teach physical education or health. If you were one of the lucky souls who had athletic aptitude, skill, or motivation, you might well have experienced a coach in action.

A good coach must first assess the strengths of the individual players and of the team as a whole. The next task is to develop a plan for improvement, taking into consideration the challenges the opposition presents and how the team functions. The coach's hopes and plans for success—winning—rely on these factors. A psychological coach follows a similar series of assessments and plans. Just as the athletic coach devises a specific set of exercises based on the athlete's key strengths, the psychological coach measures specific psychological strengths and works with the client to utilize those strengths.

In doing this, the coach draws on positive psychology, which works with the client's *strength* and is thus different from psychotherapy that focuses on symptoms and diagnoses. Positive psychology is concerned, for instance, with depression, anxiety, phobias, lack of direction, inability to develop career plans or maintain close relationships, and other related behaviors. According to the introduction to Carr's *Positive Psychology: The Science of Happiness and Human Strengths*, "Positive Psychology ... is concerned with the enhancement of happiness and well-being, involving the scientific study of the role of personal strengths and positive social systems in the promotion of optimal well-being" (Carr, 2004, p. i).

Positive psychology suggests that anyone can benefit from assessing their strengths and developing a plan for using them. It is also future-oriented in that it focuses on prevention. Positive psychology as we know it today is only 30 years old. I anticipate that as the movement continues to grow, the role of the psychotherapist is going to move closer to the coaching model. As evidence, consider the growing field of life coaching. In their book, *Therapist as Life Coach,* Williams and Davis (1998), explain that life coaches help people discover what they want in life and help them find the means to achieve it. Life coaching is, like positive psychology, directed toward the client's dreams, desires, and strengths. It is typically long-term, future-focused, and action-oriented. Psychological coaching takes the coaching model a step further. Rather than focusing on social or financial success, as do many life coaches, the psychological coach focuses on the personality strengths that make clients more resilient in the face of disappointment, tragedy, and failure.

Williams and Davis (2002) pointed out that in 1998, when life coaching started to develop as a field, society had become more fast-paced and impersonal. One of the major changes in culture that Williams and Davis identify is the widespread loss of mentors for young career-minded people. The new profession of life coaching fills that gap to some degree. The new profession of psychological coach fills that gap even more.

We are just beginning to understand and use the concept of psychological strength and psychological strength training. I believe that the role of coach is an emerging one in psychotherapy. There is a great deal of research yet to be done, but in my own quest to understand psychological strength utilization, I observed the techniques that athletic coaches use to evaluate athletes. I believe that eventually people will be able to hire psychological coaches as mentors, who will keep them focused and connected to their dreams, assist them in utilizing their strengths, and help them live their lives more purposefully.

Like today's coaches and good managers, psychotherapists can add the skills of coaching to their therapeutic toolbox. This therapeutic role focuses heavily on client strengths. An athletic coach might measure physical strength, hand–eye coordination, reaction time, speed in running, agility, the willingness to succeed and win, as well as spirit, motivation, and commitment. The psychotherapist who acts in the role of coach measures resilience, temperament, and motivation; in other words, he or she is measuring the psychological strengths of the client. He or she may also assess a client's capacity for creativity, problem-solving, hope, practicality, and other personal strengths. Assessment of such traits can help psychotherapists fortify their clients' resilience—the ability to withstand and recover from life's disappointments and tragedies.

Just as the immune system mobilizes the physical body when it's attacked by sending antibodies to the site of injury, improving blood flow, and developing even more specific antibodies to fight off infections and illness, the emotional immune system—made up of a combination of strengths—can also be shored up. The challenge of the psychotherapist functioning as a coach is to help clients identify their strengths and improve upon them, thus enhancing the ability to plan ahead and to be prepared for future stress. Even the level of a client's optimism can be increased, as Seligman demonstrates in his research with children (Seligman, 1995).

Let's follow again the actions of a coach. After a coach has identified the physical strengths of the individual athlete and the team, he or she develops a conditioning program. The program is to a degree unique for every athlete and is designed to build on the athlete's strengths. At the same time, the coach is building mental conditioning, helping athletes develop self-confidence, trust in their teammates, and an expectation of future success. With such programs, players become more optimistic about their chances to win even under the most challenging circumstances.

The conditioning process, in coaching or in psychotherapy, measures and strengthens many personal characteristics, including perseverance, focus, drive, and the need for achievement. I have developed a program that I call "Circuit Training for Life," which allows participants to identify their own strengths in these and other areas. Once their strengths are identified, participants are encouraged to practice and use them consistently. For example, imagine that you are a participant in one of these programs and have identified perseverance as a strength that needs augmentation. You might want to take up learning a second language as a practice task, since learning a language takes practice, is progressive, and has measurable results—essential elements of psychological strength-training. Such an effort might well strengthen your perseverance.

Figure 9.1 is modeled on a form that some team coaches use to record and rate their players' physiological capabilities, such as strength and speed. The form is also used to note areas that need improvement. Adapting this assessment tool for psychological strength testing, I use it specifically to evaluate the psychological strengths shown in Figure 9.1. I do this by asking clients questions or observing them in therapy. The questions are straightforward and are developed in a way that gives clients assignments between sessions. In psychotherapeutic language, this assessment sheet might be considered part of the treatment plan.

I have been consulting with a colleague who is studying to be a life coach. She has agreed to do some research on the assessment sheet, and I hope to make it an even more useful tool for psychotherapists.

Some of the same psychological strengths that I ask participants to identify in "Circuit Training for Life" are those that I use as a psychotherapist to help clients identify their strengths. Then I use the top strengths in a conditioning program. Take, for instance, the strength of persistence. Coaches work to imbue their athletes with persistence by placing them in increasingly challenging circumstances—running longer, lifting more weight, knocking more people down, catching more passes, jumping higher, and always striving to achieve more and to do so with smoother execution.

Strengths	Rating	Comments
Self-control		
Persistence		
Self-confidence		
Self-understanding		
Resilience		
Anger management		
Flexibility		
Useful aggressiveness		
Patience		
Goal-setting		
Loyalty		
Competitiveness		
Enthusiasm		
Conscientiousness		
Optimism		
Leadership		

Ratings:

9 = Significant strength; normal maintenance as needed

7 = Needs a little specific strengthening and some maintenance

5 = Needs some general strengthening and maintenance

3 = Needs significant strengthening and maintenance

1 = A major limitation; needs very significant strengthening and maintenance

Figure 9.1 Psychological Strength Assessment Sheet.

In the same way, I work as a psychotherapist to build optimism in my clients. Harmon's case is one example of how I function as a coach with clients.

Case 37: Harmon

Harmon was a 26-year-old professional golfer, referred to me by his sponsoring company, a manufacturing firm for whom I was working as a management consultant. Tall and lean, with bright eyes and a golfer's tan, Harmon had a warm, firm, friendly handshake. But under the apparent confidence and relaxed style, I could see worry, sadness, and depression. He said to me, "I'm really down, and I need to get my game back." Harmon had been doing well professionally. He was an excellent golfer, placing high in tournaments, and bringing in significant money. Now his game was off, way off.

"Do you think a psychologist can help you with your golf game?" I asked. He nodded, knowingly. "Fifty percent of golf is in your head." During our third session, Harmon told me that his brother had died in a fishing accident during the previous golf season. He said, "When he died, I had to skip a couple of tournaments to help my parents." His parents were elderly and his brother had lived with them and helped them with daily household tasks. "They were devastated and helpless," he explained, "but when I went back to the tournament circuit, my game didn't come with me. All of a sudden my golf game has gone to hell and that's my career." He was under contract with my client as a pro, and was indeed in danger of losing his job if he couldn't win tournaments.

When I told Harmon I wasn't much of a golfer, he said, "I know enough about golf for both of us." Since he didn't seem to want to talk about his brother's death yet, we talked about golf. He told me about his golfing success in college, the adoration that he garnered as a champion, his excitement at playing with prominent businessmen in his community. "It's a great life," he said, "and I used to love the game, but now I think I'm afraid of it."

Harmon told me that from college on, he had meticulously recorded every round of golf he played. He had kept records of play, drawings of golf courses—specific holes, hazards, location of the greens, and putting challenges. I asked him to bring in a few recent records, and we used them to establish what had happened to his game, stroke by stroke, putt by putt.

What we discovered was, first, that since his brother's death, he was not driving as accurately or as far as he used to. His approach shots were drifting, and he was now taking more putts. My amateur conclusion was that somehow his game had lost its power and control, and I decided to see if he could reactivate the power of his game.

I asked Harmon to spend some extra time practicing driving and going for the long ball. This part of his game quickly returned, but when we looked at his records, we realized that he was consistently putting short.

After a few sessions, Harmon was able to talk about his mentally disabled brother's death. One day, when his brother was fishing at a pond near the family farm, his fishhook became entangled in lily pads. As he walked toward the hook to loosen it, he stepped into a sinkhole and drowned. His parents blamed themselves; they were grief-stricken and lost. Harmon told me, "I had to help them. There wasn't anyone else."

We were able to relate his weakness on the golf course to the loss of his brother and the overwhelming responsibility he felt for his parents. Death and its aftermath can sap strength. I knew that for some people, depression can create a seriously weakened physical condition. We didn't talk much after that about his brother. I chose instead to focus on Harmon's game, which I felt he had the power to improve.

As he strengthened his game, his mood lifted and his depression faded. He went back to the competitive golf circuit, and I followed his career in the papers. He continued his success as a professional golfer, often appearing at the top of the leader board and winning tournaments again.

When I talked to my client, the president of Harmon's sponsoring company, he asked me for golf pointers. My one piece of advice: "Play golf with your pro." He laughed and said, "That's an interesting idea. I pay his salary, but he won't play golf with me!"

Harmon's story is, to me, a clear case of applying coaching techniques. As a psychotherapist, I became a coach by default, helping Harmon identify and utilize his natural motivation and talent in a sport. It is worth noting that we were aided significantly in Harmon's case by his golf records. I would suggest to all psychotherapists that having clients produce and share records of what is happening in their lives can be very valuable in helping them identify strengths, set goals, and work toward improvement. Using records as Harmon and I did is very similar to using maps, which I described in Chapter 2, "The Psychotherapist as Navigator." For Harmon, the records of his putting were a significant tool in his recovery, both personal and professional.

In addition to assessing strength and helping clients set goals, I use the coaching model to improve clients' motivation. Most people who come to see a therapist are looking for change. Often, it is those around them that they want to change. But at the very least, they want to "get the problem fixed." Unfortunately, not every client is motivated to work toward their own "fixing." This is not unlike the patient who consults a physician about persistent headaches and then refuses to go the distance by undergoing the recommended tests and making the necessary lifestyle changes. It's the job of the psychotherapist to identify what the client needs to do to overcome resistance and achieve his or her goals.

Case 38: Norma

A thoughtful, middle-aged woman, Norma, came to see me because, as she told me, she had conscientiously tried every diet known—Weight Watchers, low-carb diets, the Zone diet, and more—and she had lost (and then regained) only small amounts of weight. She wanted to lose 30 pounds. Her story could easily have turned out to be one more tale of a failed diet program, but for Norma, the outcome was surprisingly good.

The first thing I suggested was that we look at an important component of any good weight-loss program: exercise. "What do you do for exercise?" I asked Norma. "Well," she replied, "I do try to walk every day." She'd also joined a gym, hired a trainer, and taken up swimming. She quickly lost interest in all of these activities. Discouraged when she failed to drop pounds, she'd recently visited a bariatric clinic to ask for bypass surgery, but she had been refused because she wasn't obese enough. When I met her, she was, in her words, "desperate." She asked me, "What else can I do?"

I talked to Norma at length about her eating habits, and of course she wanted to review with me all the diet plans she had tried. It was an extensive list. "No," I said, "I want to know who you eat dinner with. How long do you spend eating lunch? Do you eat at your desk?" (She did; she ate on the fly or at her desk.) When we talked further, I learned that she had breakfast on her way to work in the car and often ordered lunch from the fast-food place across the street. At home, she raced to get her family fed so that her children could start their homework on time. She didn't see anything wrong with this. In fact, when I asked her about her own childhood mealtime experience, she admitted that her family had eaten as quickly as possible, with little conversation. A meal was just something to be gotten through.

During my assessment, Norma had demonstrated fairly clear goal-setting and even some persistence in sticking with diets. She was optimistic and motivated to lose weight, even willing to have surgery. She had a lot of stamina, and her three children were engaged in competitive sports, so she understood the concept of strength-training.

I suggested that Norma keep a journal of what she ate and when she ate it. I called this "taste-training." I also asked her to deliberately slow down her eating, taking a breath between each bite, savoring each mouthful, and starting a "taste journal" to record the experience of each meal. We agreed that she should take smaller bites, cutting everything into little pieces, and use smaller plates. I told her she shouldn't be surprised if she found that these efforts actually reduced her hunger.

I urged Norma to arrange for the family to eat together at least a few times a week, and to enhance the dining experience with conversation and music. She told me that this would be difficult, nearly impossible, because someone always had to hurry off. My question to her was, "Can you eat together as a family at least a couple of times a week?" She thought Saturday evenings and Sunday midday might be possible. I knew it was important for her entire team—her family—to learn what she was learning.

I asked her to treat eating like a sport, something to be done to the exclusion of other activities. "Just as it's impossible to do two sports at one time," I reminded her, "it's difficult to eat and do something else at the same time if you want to truly enjoy eating. So I encouraged her to leave the office for lunch, and if she did have to eat at her desk to avoid reading, checking e-mails, or doing paperwork while she ate.

I noted that many Americans like to do two or three things at once, and that this often leads to their not doing any of them well. Multitasking can also be dangerous, I pointed out. "People drive down the highway eating, drinking a soda, texting, and talking on a cell phone. If eating were to become a sport for you, then you would eat without distractions: no reading, no computer, no TV." Norma had been a competitive tennis player, so I asked her to practice eating as if she wanted to "win," which meant slowing down, tasting, and savoring meals.

We also talked about her current exercise program. How far did she walk? How long did it take her? And I asked her about her heart rate when she walked. I explained that heart rate is a good way of measuring calories consumed. She said, "I walk about 15 minutes, but I don't know how far or what my heart rate is."

"Do you really want to succeed with your weight loss program this time?" I asked her.

"Absolutely!"

"Then I want you to get a pedometer to measure how far you go, how many steps you are taking, and a finger monitor to measure your heart rate. Let's see what we can learn this week from your diet and exercise program. Do you enjoy walking?"

"Not really," she admitted.

"Then let's see if we can change that. I want you to walk fairly briskly every day for at least 30 minutes and I'd like you to be asking yourself how you can make the walk more pleasant. We need to put a little joy into your exercise program. Do you remember skipping when you were little?" I continued. "Just watching someone skip is a joy. It makes us laugh, but let's assume you can't see yourself skipping. How about practicing touch-walking? Every quarter of a mile," I explained, "you stop and touch the closest tree or the ground, using alternate hands." I felt that this exercise might help her increase her awareness of her body and her movement, and that it might make walking more pleasurable for her. I also had her keep a log of her walking.

Norma came in the following week, pleased with herself. She had her log; she had followed the diet and eaten more slowly. She had walked every day, even did a little touch-walking and recorded the distance and her heart rate. She had lost a pound and a half. Norma's weight-loss program had begun in earnest. Most important, she hadn't felt too hungry and could now envision the person she would be after she lost those 30 pounds.

When she returned the next week, she reported similar results, still not starving and almost looking forward to her walks. She did all this for the next 3 weeks: slow, small-bite eating, faster walking for longer periods of time. She was definitely working her program, so I suggested that we go to sessions once a month or as needed. Two months later, her weight loss had stopped, so we reviewed, added a little weight training, and lengthened the walking program. We also reinforced the eat-slow and small-bites sports program. This got her back on track and she was able to attain her goal.

Twenty-seven weeks later Norma came in for a "Championship Ceremony." This was, after all, a sports program. Her log showed faithful adherence to the program and a weight loss of 30.2 pounds. We reviewed her program. She went off the diet, but decided to count calories and not go over 2,200 a day, continue her walking, and weigh herself once a week, going back on her program if she gained 3 pounds. She called me recently to refer a friend and reported that she had actually lost several more pounds and that she was still slow eating and fast walking.

Case 39: Richard

Goal-setting is another activity that psychotherapists share with athletic coaches. A 20-year-old college student, Richard, came to me only because his family insisted he talk to someone before he dropped out of college. I started off by letting him know that I wasn't opposed to people dropping out of school.

"If you don't want to be there, you probably won't do very well and may flunk out. I'd rather see someone quit than be pushed out. What do you want to do rather than go to school?" I asked him.

"I don't know … bum around, drink beer, be with my friends."

"Well, I can see why your parents aren't happy about that. We need to find something for you to do that your parents can understand and accept." Notice that I said "we." I was seeing if there was a task we could agree on and a place where I could join him in the search.

"What do your parents want you to do?" I asked Richard.

"They want me to go into education and become a teacher like them."

"Well, how about that? Can you see yourself as a teacher someday?" His "no" was emphatic.

"Well," I said for the third time, "what do you see yourself doing or being someday?"

"Nothing! Absolutely nothing. I think my folks are robots, doing nothing with students who don't care. It's stupid."

"Okay, that didn't take long; it's almost as important to know what you don't want to do as it is to know what you do want to do with your life. Did you know at one time what you wanted to be?"

"Yeah," he said, "I wanted to go into medicine, but I figured I wasn't smart enough to get into med school, so I thought I'd be a nurse."

"That sounds like some good thinking to me. So?"

"So my friends all laughed and called me a girl or worse and my parents just said 'no.' So I went to college, but I feel like I'm wasting my time and my parents' dough."

"And then what happened?"

"I tried at first. I've gotten okay grades for the past 2 years, but now I'm sick of the whole thing. I'm angry at my friends, my parents, and frankly, I'm angry at myself."

"So, you're ready to give up, drop out, and just vegetate?" I asked.

"Yeah, that's about it."

"So what do you want to have happen because you came to see me today?"

"How about getting my folks off my back?" he said, smiling for the first time.

"Okay," I said, "we'll give it a try, but you have to give me an absolute pledge first."

"Yeah?" he asked sarcastically "What dumb thing do you want me to do?"

I laughed. "I'm being just like everyone else, right?"

"Right!" he nodded.

"Not quite. I know, and I think you know too, that to get your parents off your back, you have to show a little hustle." (Now I was thinking like a coach.) "We may have a chance to get your parents off your case if you come up with something—anything—constructive. And to do that, you've got to do a little work. So I want you to pledge to come see me a few times, take a few tests, and see if you can find a little direction and some goals for yourself."

"It sounds like a waste of time to me," Richard said quickly.

"It may be. So give me some idea of how you think you're going to get them off your back."

"If I knew that, I wouldn't have bothered coming to see you."

"So, consider trying my suggestion, making a pledge and giving it the old college try."

We both laughed, but not very hard.

"Okay. I pledge," Richard said. "Now what?"

"You swear to come in, take some tests, review the test results, and think about something to do as a job or career. And if you don't do these things, you promise absolutely to do something constructive around the house for the whole summer."

"I don't think I can do that."

"I repeat," I said, "keep on living with the prospect of your parents being permanently on your back for a year or two until they kick you out into the streets."

"You know," Richard said with a grin, "you almost make sense."

"Think about it and come in next week with your decision."

"No. I've decided. The pledge idea stinks, but not as bad as my parents' constant nagging. I pledge," he said, raising his hand.

"Okay," I said, "let's get to work. Come in next week. I'll have a couple of copies of the pledge for you to sign. We'll give one to your folks, which should get them off your back temporarily. During the next week I want you to talk to four or five of your buddies who are not dropping out and find out what they want to do with their lives. Will you agree to that?"

"Yes," he said, still with little enthusiasm. But it was a start. We'd formed a team with vague goals. Next week we would see if we could do a little more.

Richard came in the following week and told me that he had, in fact, talked to six of his acquaintances, but hadn't learned much. He got two major pieces of information. Two of the guys were feeling as lost and discouraged as he was. This actually cheered him up because it made him feel less alone. The others he talked to had some kind of career plan.

I then asked him to do three things: (a) Sign the pledge, (b) start taking aptitude and interest tests, and (c) go back to the people who had some kind of a career in mind, find out how they were feeling about themselves, and how they had developed their plans in the first place.

He signed the pledge and stuck the copies in his backpack. We spent the rest of the session with the Strong Vocational Interest Test. As he was leaving, he said he wasn't sure he could talk to the guys about this, but he would try. We arranged to meet again in 2 weeks, time enough to get the tests scored and for him to talk to some of his career-minded friends.

We spent most of the next session going over the test results. The vocational test confirmed his interest in medicine and expanded his thinking to include different career opportunities in the medical field: medical technician, optometrist, and respiratory therapist, as well as nurse. He also had other interests to explore: athletic trainer, auto mechanic, and photographer.

In addition to the Strong Interest Inventory (Herk and Thompson, 2002), I administered the 16PF (Catell, 1993), which measures personality traits such as openness, conscientiousness, extroversion, agreeableness, and neuroticism. I wanted to get an idea of personality factors he could mobilize to set goals and improve his life. This testing showed him to be extroverted, a concrete thinker, self-reliant, and a little tense.

Richard was pleased by most of this feedback. He was beginning to feel that maybe he could find a place for himself in the world of work and perhaps get his folks off his back. In talking to the other guys, he started to learn where their career plans had come from and he was seeing that he was on a similar course.

The vocational testing had also indicated that he wasn't at all interested in being a teacher and only moderately interested in any extended time spent in a classroom. This gave him something to show his parents and to crow about. I suggested that he talk to someone in the college's medical technology program. He actually welcomed this idea. He was becoming more positive and proactive.

This seemed a good time to ask him to do a self-review of his strengths, to complement what he had learned from the testing. He showed more enthusiasm than I had seen in him before, as he agreed to do the self-review. We scheduled a follow-up session in 2 weeks.

In this, our final session, Richard matter-of-factly presented his strengths list and his preliminary career action plan. He had found classes he was looking forward to taking in medical technology, and he enthusiastically endorsed the vocational testing to one of his friends. He had gone from a depressed near-dropout to an optimistic goal-directed young man. His mother later called to thank me, assure me that she wasn't nagging him as much, and to tell me that he seemed much happier and somewhat more career-minded. Six months later when I talked to him, he told me he was setting regular goals for himself and working at achieving them.

"Man, I'm sure glad you're my coach," he announced happily.

As you can see from these examples, the concept of psychotherapist as coach is grounded in positive psychology, and often parallels that of an athletic coach. First helping clients to identify and assess their strengths, the psychotherapist can then, through testing, learn about their motivation. The third step builds on the first two. By knowing their strengths and identifying the actions that are most likely to succeed, clients are able, with guidance, to set realistic individual goals.

Coaching has become an approach in psychotherapy that works well for some clients. Only research and time will tell what the future of the psychotherapist as coach could become. It could very well mesh with the role of the career counselor. This kind of coaching would be much like the apprenticeship programs that young people used to participate in, which gave them a chance to discover what they liked and had aptitude for before committing to a career path. The skilled artisan functioned as a coach, assessing strengths and, based on the results of performance, providing his apprentices with a skill and a livelihood. These artisans were the coaches of their day!

10 The Psychotherapist as Advertising Executive

Rebranding in Psychotherapy

For a number of years I taught a course in "Creative Thinking" at the University of Illinois-Springfield. I introduced my students to a host of ways to generate new ideas. Of the books I used as texts, one of their favorites was the father (perhaps grandfather) of these books: *Applied Imagination: Principles and Procedures of Creative Thinking* (Osborn, 1953). Osborn was a cofounder of Batten, Barton, Durstine and Osborn, one of the most influential advertising agencies of all time. In this book, Osborn makes an especially powerful argument that "man's creative ability, imagination, is ... without doubt, responsible for man's survival as an animal and it has caused him, as a human being, to conquer the world" (p. 3).

I used some of Osborn's principles to encourage my students to think outside the box, and to encourage them not to critique their ideas as they came up with them. We also used Edward de Bono's *deBono's Thinking Course* (1982). These two texts provided the foundation for my students to learn to think imaginatively.

The education of instructors as they teach is often as valuable as that of the students, and so it was with this course. I began to see correlations between encouraging students to think outside the box, and finding tools to help my therapy clients use these same free-thinking techniques to create more satisfying lives. I realized, to use advertising lingo, that I could help clients learn to "rebrand" themselves and become what they wanted to be.

Rebranding has been defined as the creation of new names, symbols, or designs for an already existing product or company. Kentucky Fried Chicken changed its identity by changing its name to KFC, thus eliminating the word *fried*, and McDonald's began competing in the designer-coffee market with reasonably priced lattes, cappucinos, frappucinos, and other 'cinos. Most recently, J.C. Penney rebranded itself as JCP and aligned itself with quality companies, while at the same time identifying themselves as a midmarket retailer rather than follow the price-reduction advertising of its competitors. These well-known companies are attempting to get consumers to see them in a new light. The actual changes in the product or company itself can be minimal. But even the smallest of changes can change how consumers perceive them. How does rebranding work as a therapeutic tool? What does it accomplish for individuals, couples, and families? How can clients' creative problem-solving generate therapeutic success? These questions lead me to suggest that the psychotherapist can help clients rebrand themselves much as an advertising executive works to rebrand a client's product or company. Rebranding is designed to change feelings, attitudes, and behaviors, whether it takes place in advertising or in the therapeutic session.

Clients usually begin therapy with a number of goals. They may want to change the way others see them, or modify their behaviors to become more at ease with themselves or the world, or more at ease themselves regarding pain and frustrations that have made them anxious, depressed, or fearful. All these goals are similar to the ones companies have when they rebrand themselves or their products. In both situations, there is a desire for change in perception.

Osborn's methods for creative thinking included what he called "change words," words that present challenges from a new perspective. Some of the words that Osborn suggested were *magnify, minimize, multiply, rearrange, adapt, combine, modify, substitute,* and *put to other uses*. Let me suggest a few more: *separate, restate, flatten, squeeze, add, subtract, freeze, protect*, and *abandon* (Osborn,1957, pp. 241–269).

Osborn saw the power of such change words in his advertising agency and in his consulting work. He believed that sensitive people who were creative and had good visualization skills could apply these capabilities to problem solving. His approach was to have the creative team define the branding challenge and imaginatively identify possible solutions through change words. In my psychotherapy practice, I adapted Osborn's approach, but broadened the scope of change words that I suggested to my clients to help them change their perceptions. These perceptions, in turn, helped clients change their behavior, seeing themselves as new and improved—or rebranded.

Case 40: Lee

Lee, a student at the university, said to me in our first session, "I can't do anything right. I'm a loser." He was living off campus, alone in a small apartment. He had no close relationships. Everything he tried seemed to backfire. When he reached out to others, he would say something inappropriate or promise to do something helpful and then completely "mess it up," in his words. The self-image he presented to me in our sessions was that of a bumbler, trying to gain approval in clumsy, unacceptable ways.

Even when Lee wasn't committing social gaffes, he was apologizing endlessly, saying "I'm sorry," over and over, sometimes for no apparent reason. Lee simply tried too hard, at the wrong time and in the wrong ways, to connect with people.

On the positive side, Lee was very bright, had an extensive vocabulary, and could come up with a bushel of ideas. He probably could have been effective as a researcher working independently. He would have driven a team crazy with his incessant apologizing.

I wanted to help channel his intensity, his creativity, and his intelligence. Neither of us expected to change his underlying personality, although some therapists might have set that as a goal. My plan was to help him rebrand himself so that he could get along more comfortably in the world. One of the resources that Lee possessed was a good imagination. He admitted, "That's the only place I can go and have any chance of success." So that's where we went.

At my suggestion, he began to apply change words to some of the challenges he had handled unsuccessfully. I asked him to use his imagination to find five small things in his life that he could change. He brought in a list of 20. I was impressed with how enthusiastically he had responded. Our initial goal was to have Lee apply a change word to each of these small things. He saw it as a game, and I agreed.

"It *is* a game," I said, "and one you can win!"

The first thing on Lee's list was the way one of his acquaintances, the closest thing he had to a friend, had treated him. This "friend" apparently reveled in Lee's social awkwardness and continually reminded him of past fiascos: "Hey, Lee, remember the time you spilled coffee all over yourself? You looked hot, ha ha!" I asked Lee to keep track of his encounters with this "friend," and to devise new words to describe the relationship. I asked Lee to "add" the benefits of the relationship and "subtract" the things in the relationship that did not make him feel good about himself. This cost–benefit study was something Lee understood. After a few sessions, he used the word *abusive* to describe the relationship. After 6 weeks of sessions, Lee's "friend" became an "acquaintance," and Lee no longer went out of his way to see him. We considered this an improvement, and Lee was ready to continue using change words.

While it may seem that eliminating his only friend from his life was not the best way to improve his already inferior social skills, it made it possible for Lee to clear the decks for the possibility of a genuine friendship and to escape an abusive relationship. After he applied change verbs to the challenges in his life for a while, Lee seemed more at ease and told me that as he put more distance between him and his acquaintance, he began to feel better about himself. "You know," he told me, "by adding and subtracting the pluses and minuses of the relationship, I have learned to almost like myself for the first time." He began to imagine what it would be like to have a real friend or two, and what it would be like not to constantly be apologizing.

Lee began spending more time with new acquaintances. Several became friends. He would assist them with research or suggest topics for papers they wanted to write. He used his newly discovered creativity to help his friends gain new perspectives. Because he was being helpful, and not "messing things up," he was appreciated.

Lee now had a small hope that he could make his life better. He chose new change words, "separate" and "squeeze," to address the boredom he was facing at school. "Squeezing" his possibilities let him take on new challenges. When one of his new friends asked him to do something, he would "squeeze" the idea to determine whether it fit his talents and strengths. If it did, he would take on the challenge with zest and enthusiasm. If after "squeezing" the idea he felt it was a bad fit, he would say no. After a few more sessions, Lee chose to continue his change-word project on his own. Applying change words had changed Lee's point of view, and he continued to feel better about himself.

Case 41: Warner and Maggie

Another case in which I employed the idea of change words was with a middle-aged couple, Warner and Maggie. They had each been married before and both described their first marriages as "just falling apart for no reason." Their first spouses had become disenchanted and asked for divorces. Warner and Maggie had met just 18 months later, and within 6 months they got married. Neither had children and both of them made decent livings and were careful with their money. After 6 years, their main complaint was that their marriage was suffering from neglect. "We just don't have anything to do together or say to each other. We don't even seem to have a relationship anymore," they told me. They saw vacations as too expensive, and even resisted the weekend getaway I suggested.

We began with the questions I usually ask couples. When did you first meet? What did you do on your first date? What did you think and feel about each other during those early times? When did the relationship get serious? What was happening when you got engaged? What was the marriage ceremony like? The honeymoon? And then what? While they cooperated with the exercise, most of their responses to me were unenthusiastic. So I probed further.

I thought the change word concept might be useful in this case. So I put a collection of change words in a paper sack and had each of them draw one and keep it in mind as they interacted for the next week. Neither knew what word the other had. I asked both to pay attention to any changes in the relationship and to be prepared to bring in a review of the week for the following session. I even asked them to guess what word their partner was using. I was hoping that this would be a way to encourage them to think about each other, which I suspected they had not been doing. Because this couple had created so little adventure for themselves, they were actually excited about this idea and looked forward to the challenge. I recalled a quote from Osborn's book: "Kiss and make up may work fine at first, but later after runs up against the law of diminishing returns, a far better rule is to 'kiss and think up'" (1953, p. 45).

The first two words they selected were *rotate* for Maggie and *curious* for Warner. The following week, when the couple returned, Maggie told me that she was pleased with how they had interacted with each other for the past week. She had been feeling neglected for years because Warner didn't show any interest in her, but that week he had asked her every day about her plans and her activities. "He really showed a lot of interest. His word must have been "aware," she said. We all laughed when he corrected it to "curious." He had been trying to find out how she felt about him and their marriage for years, he explained. His interest in her day-to-day activities began to make a real difference in their relationship.

Then I asked Warner to describe what he had experienced. He responded that he had always been annoyed with her superior attitude when they disagreed. "She has always treated me as if I don't know all the facts. Maybe we both think she is smarter than I am. Her grades were better in school, but this past week she's treated me like an equal intellectually and that's made me feel less defensive."

Warner turned to his wife, took her hand, and said, "Thank you. Maybe your word was 'equal.'"

"No," she said. "If I'd known what you had been feeling I would have tried to fix it years ago. But my word was 'rotate.'" He was bewildered, and so was I. I asked Maggie to explain.

"Well," she declared, "the word puzzled me. How do you "rotate" your behavior? I almost rejected the word and asked for another, but then I decided to try it out. It was hard, because every time we came together and I needed to use it I had to pause and think, 'How do I rotate that?' which caused me to hesitate and be uncertain."

Her hesitancy and uncertainty made Warner realize that she had doubts and insecurities too. Warner responded, "And I took that as your attempt to treat me like an equal, which made things better for both of us." I asked them if they would like to continue with two new words. This time her word was *magnify* and his was *wash.* I asked them to continue using their original words and to add these new words. I encouraged them to continue to guess what their partner's new word might be.

The next week we had another session that included good humor and laughter, which I considered progress. Warner decided that "wash" actually might mean more showers and baths. He explained that his wife sometimes complained that he had come to bed unshowered, so he needed to be more conscientious about his personal hygiene. Maggie explained that she didn't feel he was dirty, but that he would get into bed after watching a football game with the guys and drinking too much beer. "You smelled a little too much like a beer hall," she said.

"You mean I didn't have to take all those showers?" Warner retorted, and they both laughed. Then he asked her an important question for both of them: Did the beer smell turned her off sexually? When she admitted it had, he resolved out loud, "Less beer, more sex!" Although they had been reluctant to discuss their sex life, they were able to use their change words to create more intimacy.

Since their relationship seemed to be moving toward intimacy, I urged them to set aside time to discuss what would make each of them feel and be more loving, affectionate, and sexual. I asked what she had thought his second word was. She said since he was being more attentive to her feelings, she thought it was *attention*. Maggie's second word was *magnify*. Every time she became aware of something thoughtful that he was doing, she magnified it and complimented him. He told her that he thought her word had been *affection*, which we all agreed was a good thing to magnify. They both agreed that they had come a long way from the indifference and neglect that had originally brought them to therapy.

I had each of them select one more word, to prevent relapse. This time, they were agreeable, even enthusiastic. I had them choose their own word, which they would then use for the week. Maggie chose *tender* and Warner chose *caring*.

The week that followed, they told me, was almost like their dates before they got engaged. They were joyful, caring, thoughtful, and loving. They both treasured what they had regained. They terminated therapy with a pledge to each other to never get so busy and preoccupied that they would neglect their relationship again.

Alex Osborn would have been very pleased. He said, "Imagination is not only 'of the essence,' but can be the key to successful marriages" (1953, p. 46).

One of the most significant areas in which change words can help clients redefine or rebrand themselves is the arena of family therapy and parenting. An important idea from *Applied Imagination* relates to parenting: "If we parents could only nudge instead of nag!" Osborn laments. "Nagging takes only a tongue, but nudging calls for creative thinking" (1953, p. 46).

Let me illustrate the idea of rebranding with a story about my own family. When our oldest daughter, Mary, was about 4 years old, she wanted to help with the dishes. My wife gave her a dish towel and smilingly asked her to dry a couple of the smaller plates. You would have enjoyed watching this blond, blue-eyed happy little girl, busy and intense with the effort. Everything went well until the fourth plate, wet and slick, slipped from her small hands, dropping and breaking.

Both my wife and I reacted angrily, and Mary ran to her room crying. We finished the dishes in silence. Later my wife and I talked, and out of that discussion came a family rule that we have adhered to ever since: "In our family, if you are trying to help you can't get in trouble!" No matter what it was or who did it, the family rule held. It became a mantra throughout the years. We rebranded the family as one in which no one could get in trouble as long as they were trying to be helpful.

While the environment of the family and that of a large company are very different, rebranding can be applied to both. In times of corporate restructuring, mergers, liquidations, layoffs and other activities that define modern corporate life, management consultants are often asked to take an assignment that the company leadership doesn't want to do—like the messy, gut-wrenching job of firing someone. In the 2011 movie *Up in the Air*, George Clooney is the management consultant called in to do the dirty work. When I saw the movie, I was reminded of the 5 years that I spent as a management psychologist. While I can't flatter myself that I had George Clooney's charm, I tried to be as imaginative and diplomatic as possible when I had dirty work to do.

Case 42: "Colonel" George and Henry

I was a consultant to "Colonel" George, president and owner of a successful and expanding family business. After I had been working with his company for about 6 months, he told me that he wanted a favor from me. (Note to management psychologists: When you are a consultant, and asked to do a favor, you're probably going to be doing something unpleasant.) One of their employees, Henry, had been with the company since it was founded by Colonel George's father, some 30 years earlier. Henry was promoted as the company grew, but the current executive team did not feel he was providing the leadership the company needed. Naturally, they didn't want to tell him this, so my assignment was to find a place for Henry where his experience and his willingness to "look after things," as Colonel George's dying father had asked him to do, could be put to use.

Colonel George had already talked to Henry several times and knew that Henry had no plans for retiring any time soon. The Colonel was under pressure from the executive team to get Henry out of the management group, and he asked me to find a way to do that. Pressuring Henry to retire was an option that would have repercussions for the Colonel. Henry had a loyal following among long-time employees. If there was an alternative, the Colonel was open to it. He had put off a decision about what he called "the Henry problem" for a year. He said to me, "As a consultant, you're the best guy to do this." This statement was almost enough to make me consider leaving the consulting business. No one was going to come out ahead—not Henry, Colonel George, or me. That evening I flew home and talked to my boss, who reminded me that such situations are why companies hire consultants. I went to my office with a heavy heart. It was clear to me that, as they say in the advertising world, I was going to have to "sell what no one was buying."

I called Colonel George the next day and asked him to schedule a meeting with Henry and his wife, Gloria, the following week. I had met Henry and Gloria several times and knew that they functioned as a team. My goal was to explore carefully what this couple wanted and reconcile their desires with the company's intentions for Henry. Henry and Gloria were anxious about the meeting and worried that Henry would be forced into retirement. Gloria wanted Henry to retire, but didn't want him to lose face. Their first words to me were, "What bad news do you have for us?"

"Before we talk about that," I said, "I need to know what you two want to do in the years ahead." With that, Gloria burst into tears. "Henry still wants to stay with the company," she said, "and I want him to retire. The last few years in the company have been hell on earth for us. Henry knows that some members of the executive team aren't happy with him, and he doesn't understand what they want from him. When George's father was dying, Henry promised him that he would take care of the company, and that's what he has been trying to do. But it's killing him and me too."

I spent a great deal of time that day comforting them. Then I complimented Henry on his promise to take care of the company and asked the two of them to give me some time to find a solution that would satisfy everyone—Henry, Gloria, the Colonel, the executive team, and the company. At the same time, I wanted to support Henry's promise to take care of the company. My job was to rebrand Henry and sell his new image and role to the executive team. I was going to have to package this concept pretty nicely to sell it.

I did what any good advertising executive might do in the same situation. I went to a nearby cafeteria, ordered a cup of coffee, and started doodling on my napkin, listing possible solutions. I can tell you from experience that many good advertising concepts and branding ideas have their birth on those paper napkins. I saw the Colonel that afternoon. He anticipated that I was going to tell him to retire or fire Henry, and he dreaded having to do either one. But the look on his face changed from dread to relief as I told him what I had in mind.

I proposed a special advisory committee, appointed by him, consisting of Henry and two respected recent retirees. The committee would meet on an as-needed basis (whenever they felt like it) and discuss just one topic: "What could the company do to improve business?" The arrangement would be open-ended and would give Henry free rein to look after the business. It would also get him off the executive team, which would please his wife.

I suggested that Henry stay on the payroll as the liaison to the committee, at the same money he would have drawn at retirement, and that the formation of the committee be announced at a party, thrown in appreciation of Henry's 30 years of service to the company. I learned later that the executive team was willing to go along with this plan, as long as Henry was out of management.

I did get to go to the appreciation party, where Gloria took me aside and thanked me 10 times over. I realized that when the consultant gets dropped in the swamp he might just come back with a handful of orchids, if he can be imaginative.

One thing puzzled me at first. After the resolution of "the Henry problem," I was welcomed at the company as a friend, whereas before I was greeted as a dirty-deed doer, a hired gun. In fact, I was neither. What I had done was to rebrand Henry in a way that everyone accepted, and in the process had rebranded myself. That's a better outcome than most consultants can ask for!

Case 43: Rob

I found it to be as true in psychotherapy as Osborn did in advertising that sometimes tiny changes can add a great deal to a thing, or in the case of psychotherapy, to an individual. In my early days as a counselor at the University of Missouri, I was just starting to develop my therapeutic skills. I was still learning how to conduct a therapeutic inquiry, and to adjust my pace to the client's mind-set. I was able to help one client, Rob, make small, nonthreatening changes that had an immediate effect, and that eventually led to larger life changes.

Rob, a freshman at the university, was having trouble making friends and adjusting to campus life. He was the only child of a well-to-do-family and grew up on a small farm where, for a number of years, he was home-schooled. He was smart, nice looking, sensitive and shy, very shy.

I couldn't help noticing that his interpersonal skills were limited. He talked haltingly and had trouble making eye contact, and he told me he was easily overwhelmed on a large campus. This was clearly a case where timing was of the essence. How was I to help him plunge into the hot water of college life—making friends, socializing, and even dating—without sending him into a panic? If I moved too quickly, he could be blocked by his own anxiety. If I moved too slowly, he might freeze and drop out of school, so great was his apprehension and social uncertainty.

As he told me about his almost complete inexperience with women and of his discomfort during male smut talk, I wondered if his sexual orientation was part of his anxiety. What he told me about his dorm-mates' teasing made me wonder if they thought he was gay and whether they were trying to "smoke him out."

I could have delved into Rob's close relationship with his mother, or his sexual identity, but instead I wanted to help him find situations where he could learn basic social skills and become more comfortable around his classmates. I referred him to the community-campus volunteer program. The Volunteer Center found a placement for him that I felt could be excellent for him. So with some considerable encouragement on my part, he began to volunteer at a retirement community near the campus. His reception there was immediate and positive. He was comfortable with older people and really enjoyed helping them. He played cards with residents, ran errands for them, and even did their shopping. He also proved to be a very good listener.

These activities helped him build effective social skills. He developed enough self-confidence to chat almost comfortably with the coeds who also volunteered there. He even dated one of them. For Rob, the "therapeutic work" of building effective interpersonal skills was accomplished at the retirement community. Psychotherapy can take a lot of different forms.

I saw Rob a couple of years later on campus, and he introduced me to his girlfriend. She was an attractive, bubbly redhead who greeted me as if I were a long-lost friend. I never found out what he had told her about our therapeutic relationship. It didn't matter. The fact was that I helped Rob rebrand himself by just a little tweaking, applying Osborn's notion of changing "one tiny thing."

Note: The students in my "Creativity" class especially liked the four books that I used as texts:

- *Applied Imagination: Principles and Procedures of Creative Problem-Solving,* by Alex F. Osborn (1953). This book is currently out of print. However, if you can find a collector's or library copy, you will discover that it laid the groundwork, in its first printing in 1953, for the three books that follow, and many others that address the creative process.
- *Conceptual Blockbusting: A Guide to Better Ideas,* by James Adams (1994), because it is so concise and offers such a good understanding of the blocks to solving problems, this is a major source.
- *de Bono's Thinking Course,* by Edward de Bono (1982), because it gave them an interesting way to become better thinkers.
- *Universal Traveler: A Guide to Problem Solving and the Process of Reaching Goals,* by Dan Koberg and Jim Bagnall (2003), a fun book that has more than a hundred guides, tools, and diagrams designed to help people become more creative.

11 The Psychotherapist as Conservationist

Does the concept of conservation have meaning and value in a discussion about psychotherapy? I believe it has a great deal to offer and in fact it may play a significant part in the future of psychotherapy. One of the editors of *Hands-on Nature* (Lingelbach & Purcell, 1986/2000), Lisa Purcell, told me in an e-mail, "Sustainability means understanding that resources are limited and precious, and are our gift to the future." I doubt the reader will disagree with me when I suggest that psychological resources are limited. If we squander or waste our personal psychological resources, it is as if we had overmined coal or overgrazed a meadow. It is one of the ways people put themselves at risk for psychological damage.

When I talk about wasting personal resources, I am talking about behaviors like taking dangerous drugs, seriously abusing alcohol, driving recklessly, losing our tempers, setting unreasonable goals, and allowing anxiety, fear, or depression to run our lives. Framing wasting personal resources in this way demonstrates that there are a number of ways that individuals can use or rather misuse their personal resources to their own detriment. It makes sense that a personal conservation program might help with the sustainability of personal resources. In Chapter 6, "The Psychotherapist as Engineer," there is a chart that reflects two very distinct areas of activity. The first area has an array of activities that can increase psychological energy. The second area is full of activities that conserve the psychological energy that has been generated (Figure 6.2).

There are demonstrated and accepted ways to generate greater psychological energy. We review many of them in Chapter 6 because engineers are specifically responsible for generating energy. The second area, methods of conserving or saving energy, is covered in this chapter as the psychotherapist as conservationist is explained.

In Figure 11.1, you will see five areas of activities that I teach to clients. These activities, 27 in all, can help clients conserve psychological energy. Part of the reason that these activities work is that they reduce stress, one of the greatest drains on psychological energy.

1. Developing More Effective Coping Skills

- Assertiveness Training
- Active Listening
- Conflict Resolution Skills.

2. Avoid Gaming Behaviors

- Game Analysis
- Avoiding Discounts
- Avoid the Rescue Triangle
- Avoid Power Plays
- Script Work.

3. Desensitization Training

- Reducing Fears
- Reducing Angers
- Reducing Frustrations
- Reworking Guilt Feelings
- Reducing Doubling and Insecurity.

4. Productive Skills Training

- Time Management and Pacing
- Planning and Organizing
- Decision Making
- Prioritizing
- Delegation
- Supervision.

5. Stress Reduction Techniques-Training

- Breathing Exercises
- Relaxation Techniques
- Autogenic training
- Meditation Training
- Psycho-Imagery
- Visualization Training
- Practice Surrender Control
- Worry Workshop.

Figure 11.1 Conservation Activities for Psychotherapy.

It is up to the psychotherapist using this model to ensure that clients sustain the resources that they have and are building along the way. A good psychotherapist always helps clients identify possible drains and demands on their energy, and teaches them to plan ahead. Prevention of loss is one of the keys to good conservation, and it's as important in psychotherapy as it is in conservation.

My time in the Counseling Center at the University of Missouri gave me ample opportunity to function as a psychoconservationist. A case that comes to mind is that of Tony, who had begun his education behind bars.

Case 44: Tony

Tony was a 20-year-old who had done time for trafficking in drugs. He had only served 2½ years of his 5-year sentence due to good behavior. Now a student at the university, he was referred to the Counseling Center by one of his professors, who recognized a smart young man who was making very little academic progress.

When Tony first swaggered into my office, he was unshaven. His hair was sticking up in spikes, and his eyes were red-rimmed, as if he hadn't slept. He was tall and rangy and dressed in dirty jeans and a torn, tattered t-shirt. Tony had the look of a diminished young man.

When I reviewed his life with him, I learned that his family relationships had been chaotic. His father had been in prison for robbery. His mother was an alcoholic. He grew up running with a drug gang in a mid-sized town. He discovered an appreciation of marijuana early in life, and it became a demanding habit. As his usage increased, he needed money. From his point of view, the only reliable source of income was dealing drugs. He knew who the big dealers were, and he knew he could get an extra supply of drugs, sell them, and still afford his habit. As a junior dealer, he was the more exposed and one of the first in his neighborhood to get busted. Caught in a raid with a more than ample supply, he was quickly arrested, tried, and sentenced.

When I first met with Tony, he told me how lost he felt. "I don't know whether I'm shit or Shinola," he said. "At one time I felt on top of the world. I was high all the time. I was selling lots of pot, and what I couldn't sell I smoked. Man, that was the life." He recounted the glory days to me. Just before he got out of high school, he was a successful dealer. He had money in his pocket, a car, nice clothes, several girlfriends, and the respect of his peers. As a senior in high school and a successful dealer, he was in a good position to recruit new users. His skill in recruiting users helped him develop interpersonal skills that we were later able to use to his advantage.

Even in prison, Tony had some respect: "My homeboys in prison, they were solid," he said. "They had my back." Tony was able to use the prison's educational resources to become a successful student by prison standards. He earned an associates' degree with moderately good grades. He knew what he was supposed to do, and the prison system built in plenty of time for him to read the assigned books and write the required papers. As a good student in prison, he gained the respect of his teachers. He almost felt like a dealer again, but this time he was pushing education instead of drugs. He said, smiling, "Education is a lot like drugs. If you can get a supply and get turned on, life is good."

What Tony and I discovered was that it was a lot easier for him to control his life and manage his time in jail than it was in an apartment on campus. As a consequence, his grades were very low. He was failing most of his courses. He spent his time drinking beer with his buddies. More importantly, he had begun to smoke pot again, looking over his shoulder for the parole officer who periodically showed up. As a college student, he was able to snow his parole officer, but he had to stay on his toes. My job was to help Tony draw on his available resources and find a way for him to deploy them legally to his advantage.

The psychotherapist as conservationist needs to know what resources are available. I needed to help Tony find out what his aptitudes, interests, and academic strengths were. I administered extensive aptitude and achievement tests. The tests told us that he was intellectually capable of doing college-level work. However, he was lacking in life organization and academic skills. His writing was disorganized; he was unable to manage his time. His reading was at a sixth-grade level, which was adequate for a prison setting, where he had plenty of time. With the pressures and demands of a college setting, however, a sixth-grade reading level, along with many distractions, made it impossible for Tony to keep up with his homework assignments. His sixth-grade reading level provided neither the level of comprehension nor the speed he needed to do college-level work.

Tony and I spent time identifying his personal resources, including his intelligence and his competitive nature. These were valuable traits but they contributed to his overconfidence. He thought he could achieve in college in the same flashy way that had worked for him in prison. Now, his lack of academic skill and lack of self-discipline were holding him back. In terms of the conservation metaphor, his resources were quickly being drained.

One of the important things I did to help Tony shore up his resources was to refer him to the Learning Center on campus. After a month's work at the Learning Center, he was referred to an individual tutor, as well. He resisted these efforts at first, but, then became cooperative as he saw the value of these efforts. The resources provided by the University ultimately helped him develop his study skills and boosted his reading level so that he could keep up with his work. I continued to work with him into the next semester. His grades improved, and I encouraged him to use his well-developed recruiting skills. As a peer counselor, he was able to steer other students to the resources he had used—the Counseling and Learning Centers. This built his self-confidence, and helped him revitalize and conserve his skills and energy.

I was able to function as a psychotherapist as conservationist with a number of other students during my time at the University of Missouri. Many had not come out of controlled settings like prison, but rather out of environments where there was no control.

Case 45: Bobby

Bobby rarely completed his class assignments. But that was the least of his problems. He was living in chaos, not cleaning up after himself, and getting into shouting matches with his roommates. It's no surprise that Bobby didn't self-refer but was referred by his mother. She was worried about his grades and concerned that he was about to be kicked out of student housing.

When I met with him, Bobby was immaculately dressed in a starched shirt and pressed pants. His loafers gleamed. He was clean-shaven and neat. His smile was the product of expensive orthodontia. His manners were polite, with a touch of arrogance. He fully expected help to be provided with little effort from him. He said, "My mom and dad think that the university isn't giving me the help I need."

"What is it that you think you need?" I asked him. He said he didn't know.

"How are you doing?" I asked.

"Well so far, I'm getting D's. I will probably have to repeat some of my classes." He shrugged, as if it didn't matter. I asked him how much time he was spending on class preparation. He looked at me blankly and said, "Well, I thought going to class was really enough, and I almost always go. That's what I did in high school, and it worked okay. What more do these instructors want?"

I asked, "Don't some of these courses require homework?" Smiling slyly, he said, "Oh, I can usually buy whatever papers I need."

I learned that Bobby's SAT scores were high. His parents paid for two SAT preparation courses and had him take the test twice. His high school GPA was slightly above average, but he admitted that his mother had written a lot of his papers. His high school teachers expected him to do good work. They didn't recognize that he was just sliding by.

As an only child, with a doting mother, aunt, and grandmother, Bobby had to do little or nothing for himself. As a college freshman, he was still taking his laundry home every other weekend. If he was too busy to go home, he sent his laundry home with a friend. When he lived at home, his mother made his bed and cleaned his room. His father gave him a car for his 16th birthday and had it washed for him every other week. He had gone out for sports, but he told me that the coaches "were on me all the time to put more into it, so I quit." Being an athlete was too hard, he said. He had a dream of being a star halfback, but neither his athletic ability nor his work ethic was sufficient to achieve this dream. After a few weeks of what he considered needless sweating and effort, he dropped out of football and then basketball. He didn't even bother going out for baseball.

Bobby's problem was that he had innate talents and resources, but he didn't know how to use them wisely or conserve them for when he needed them. It was clear that his highly motivated and organized parents had enabled Bobby. Not only did he have poor study skills, he had no self-discipline. His life skills were very limited; he had never washed or maintained a car, bought a new printer, or cleaned a refrigerator. Even his grandmother acknowledged he was "bone-lazy."

The first thing I did was arrange for Bobby to take a university mini-course called "Improving Study Skills." It provided him with some tools for working in a university environment. His tutor insisted that Bobby do his own work and stay on a daily study schedule. Bobby did only what he absolutely had to do. He tried very hard to manipulate his tutor into providing more and more help, but the tutor held her ground.

Bobby came back to see me after one frustrating encounters with his tutor, who wisely resisted his trap. I helped the bewildered Bobby realize that he was expending so much energy trying to get others to do his work for him that he had little time, focus, or energy left to learn. Bobby was a classic case of someone who needed to learn conservation practices, and part of my job as a conservationist was to help him take an inventory of his resources and guide him toward using them wisely and more productively.

Over the course of the semester, Bobby began to break some of his bad habits. He discovered that there was a certain satisfaction in completing something by himself. My clue to his progress was that his complaints about his tutor lessened as he was forced to do more for himself. He passed his courses that semester, but not by much. On the positive side, his parents told me that when he came home on break, he made his bed, washed his own car, and even took out the trash when asked. They were delighted at the change in him and asked me what kind of miracles we had performed at the university. In reality, what Bobby and I had done together was to start him on a path of true resource management.

He himself was disappointed in his grades. His expectations had been unrealistic, as they were for everything. When he began looking for a major he discovered business management. I suspected that he thought that a manager was someone who made other people do the work. He still thought he deserved the best of everything whether or not he earned it. But slowly he began to realize that to get what he wanted, he had to apply himself. Using his own resources was a monumental shift for him. Ultimately he blamed me for his tutor's intransigence in helping him, but he also admired it. He said, "Dr. Miller, I'm wise to you. What you have been trying to get me to do is do my own work. Isn't that true?"

I smiled and said, "Bobby, I honestly believe if you exercise your brain muscle, it will strengthen it!" He smiled back, and said, "Unfortunately, I think you're right."

Bobby's ingratiating personality and newfound motivation eventually led him to major in business management. While he never became a top performer, he had found a conserved pool of resources that he could draw upon to finish school.

Sometimes, conservation lessons can be short term, while their outcomes are lifelong and dramatic. I have had opportunities to create, in my practice and my university teaching, communities for conservation. A stress reduction program that I organized at the university is an example.

Case 46: Agnes, Sally, Dolores, Elizabeth, and Mary Jane

The opening of a senior university—seniors, juniors, and graduate students—in our town attracted many mature women who had dropped out of college to marry and raise families and were now returning to complete their degrees. Often, such women worried that they would not be able to cope with the demands of college and the competition with younger students. They were not sure that they still knew how to study and learn, and were especially anxious about the tests that they would have to take.

I met with several groups of these women to begin building their confidence and to change their perception of a test from enemy to study guide and "almost friend." The youngest of the original group of three, Agnes, had two children in junior high. She had been out of school for nearly 15 years. Short and stocky with graying hair, Agnes was a dynamo and quickly became the de facto leader of the group. But some of her energy was being siphoned off by her fear of taking tests. Her ultimate fear was that she would be handed a test to take, and her mind would go completely blank. Agnes's worst nightmare was that she would remember only her name, and leave the rest of the test blank.

Two other women in this group were slightly older and had grown children. They were also test-fearful. One of them, Sally, had been told that she was dyslexic in second grade. She had never forgotten that, and it contributed to her test anxiety. I referred her briefly to the Learning Center, where she was reassured to discover that her reading skills were more than adequate for college. Dolores, the third woman, had never seen herself as a student. Her desire, as she described it, was to be "a good mommy." Her plan had been to be a home economics teacher. Now she found herself back in school with the ultimate goal of getting a bachelor's degree in home economics, and maybe even teaching that subject. For her, academic performance had never been as important as her homemaking dream.

Two more return-to-schoolers joined the group later. The fourth one, Elizabeth, who had been called Betty but now called herself Liz, explained that her nickname was one of the things she was doing to reinvent herself. (We might want to think of this as part of Liz changing her life narrative.) The fifth woman, Mary Jane, told me she found it boring to keep a house as clean as her engineer husband wanted it to be. Her goal was to finish school, find a well-paying job, and hire a housekeeper. She was currently struggling with the guilt her husband had been laying on her about her so-so housekeeping skills. In addition to reducing her fear of tests, we also worked on reducing her pseudoguilt. Both were draining her energy and were unproductive, so we put some conservation in place.

These five women had met in a class and were all very focused on their academic performance. Their biggest collective fear, as midterm exams loomed, was that after years of insisting that their children get good grades, they might not be able to perform in an academic setting themselves. My job as conservationist was to convene this little conservation community, help them identify their existing resources, and help them reduce their anxiety about taking tests.

I met with the group regularly. They agreed almost immediately that their mutual task was helping each other through the first fearful semester of school. As they discussed their experience of being back in a university setting, they shared their life stories with the group. It quickly became clear that they were very capable group of women. They had done well in high school, maintaining above-average GPAs. A brief preliminary test that I administered to them indicated that their academic skills were more than adequate. They had good reading and writing capabilities. They quickly recognized their ability to do college-level work, despite their shared anxiety about testing.

You may wonder why five such competent women were so worried about test-taking. It was true that they had been away from academics for some time, which could have made them uneasy. But one of the key sources of test anxiety is a student's experience in grade school. Almost all grade-school children worry about not knowing the right answers. Everyone can remember a classmate who complained of a stomach ache when a test was coming up. And that fear is contagious. When you ask grade-school children what they are scared of, many will identify taking tests as a very fearsome experience. Parents typically do little to dispel their children's' fear of testing, oftentimes completely dismissing their children's worries, saying, "Don't worry. You'll do fine."

With their fear of testing, these five competent women may as well have been back in first grade. I knew that feedback was essential to improving performance, and that improved performance reduces anxiety. First, I asked each of them to build a test based on the materials they were studying and believed they would be tested on. They could use reading materials, old tests, teachers' guidelines, and anything else they thought would be helpful. In other words, I charged our conservation community with the task of identifying a pool of external resources, one of the key tenets of conservation.

Once these external resources had been accessed, we pursued another tenet of conservation, putting resources to more efficient use. We used the information we had gathered to build a test, and the group actually took their own tests. They all did astonishingly well. I was not surprised, and they were all pleased. While these self-made tests were still not friends, they were far less threatening. The women were now better prepared for the challenges of academic life. We repeated the test-building exercise several times to reinforce the first success and to help them become even more prepared for the upcoming midterm.

Between the midterm and the posting of test results, I worried that I might have been overconfident and set the women up for failure. I thought to myself, "My God! I've contracted Test Terror!" But it turned out that their midterm grades were fine: three A's, a B and a B–. The women were all smiles, and I relaxed. They now knew that they could do college work and that tests were no longer something to be dreaded.

At our next-to-last session, I told them they had earned their diplomas from BYTTCU. When they looked puzzled, I explained: "Building Your Test-Taking Confidence University." I asked them to build and bring in their own diplomas, just as they had built their own tests and their own confidence. At the last session, they "graduated" and we had a party. I might add that there were some interesting diplomas. Sally, the woman who had thought she was dyslexic, used a very formal style for her diploma, printing it in big, neat, letters. Dolores, hoping to be an home economics teacher, had a diploma with a big painted hand on it, which she said was her own hand patting herself on the back. Liz's was beautifully designed, with a flowery border and official-looking type. They had all put effort into their diplomas, just as they had worked so hard to convert tests from terror to friend.

The graduation ceremony we held was a significant part of the "conservation therapy." It was a way to recognize the women's good test scores and encourage them to conserve their new-found confidence and skills. In conservation, we make changes toward more productive behavior with sustainability, which emphasizes the ability to endure and maintain. Stewardship, another key conservation concept, has to do with taking care of what has been given to us. By graduating and leaving their test-terror behind, these women were able, as a community, to sustain and build upon their self-confidence.

We disbanded the group, which had served its purpose, but each of the women checked in with me periodically. I had the pleasure of following their progress in their college careers. They all did well and attended graduation with their families in the audience. Two of them went on to graduate school and earned advanced degrees.

The conservation principles of psychotherapy lend themselves particularly well to a group setting. This is not surprising, since the concept of land, water, and animal conservation always requires community effort and support. It is largely the energy of the whole that replenishes individual resources. In return, those individuals, fortified, are able to give back to the whole. Isn't that the whole point of education and of conservation?

In each of these case examples, I functioned as a conservationist in an academic environment. A university or college is in its own way a conservation entity, providing resources and guidance on how to use those resources. Just as people who want to preserve endangered species might look to the World Wildlife Fund, or those concerned about national parks might follow the principles of the Sierra Club, the university student is offered a model of conservation. To paraphrase the well-known adage, the university not only teaches students to fish, but shows them where the lake is and how to bait their hooks. Now *that's* conservation!

12 The Psychotherapist as Research Psychologist

In order to advance the field of psychotherapy, we need to continue the research initiated in the 1960s. This research was comprised of a series of investigations of the fundamentals and procedures in psychotherapy. As I look at the current publications in the field, even those as recent as January and February of 2012, I have become increasingly aware that research in the field has provided extensive information about the field. This research tells us that the standard approach of the 50-minute hour and the one-on-one relationship is fine. However, research is now suggesting that this approach is not always adequate.

In 2010, the New York State Psychological Association (NYSPA) organized a think tank whose intention was to ask what health care, including mental health care and psychotherapy, would be like after statutes such as the Patient Protection and Affordable Care Act (PPACA) were passed. The product of this think tank was the New York State Psychological Association's Tool Kit on Health Care Reform. Among the areas addressed were a focus on quantitative outcomes. The Toolkit, available online, addresses the need for research: "Health reform will include data driven expertise and the need for clinical outcome data. We are living in an era in which quantitative analysis will be critical to have available when tough decisions need to be made about where to allocate limited funds. For this reason, it is important to be able to read and digest the most current research in psychology. This will allow psychologists who work primarily as clinicians to back practice with data-driven arguments and to continue to have a seat at the table when it comes to treatment of patients" (NYSPA Tool Kit for Health Reform, 2011).

As health care reform takes place, we have our work cut out for us. Every practitioner in the mental health field will be part of this enormous shift, but the role of research and the research psychologist will be particularly significant. Investigations will have to be made into the types and diversity of assessment tools before, during, and at the completion of psychotherapeutic treatment; significant research will be required to determine how to achieve successful outcomes, possible relapses, and to identify additional treatment resources. A huge number of studies will be conducted to establish empirically supported treatment for diverse populations of clients. As an example, specific treatments will have to be identified for different demographics and ages of clients, including infants, geriatric patients, and the chronically ill, the physically handicapped, the chronic and emotionally mentally ill, the prison population, the military, the economically disadvantaged, the multilingual population, ethnic minorities, lesbian, gay, bisexual, and transgender clients.

Most important is the shift In paradigm from treatment to prevention. Alternate delivery systems will have to be designed, evaluated, and put in place. For example, treatment programs that are media-delivered may emerge. In working with families, child development and behavior will have to be investigated.

As all the implications of this paradigm shift are considered, we must also think about the training, consultation, and education required for such changes to transform mental health care. To understand the scope of these changes, it may be helpful to review several cases that involved research psychology in the current delivery of services. The first case examines one of psychotherapy's most important elements, the relationship between the psychotherapist and the client, and questions some of the assumptions about that relationship.

Case 47: Adam

Some years ago, when I was teaching at the University of Illinois at Springfield, I had a dynamic and successful colleague. He was well-liked by all of us and well-known in the community. When I met him, Adam had just begun teaching at the university. He had already made a name for himself as an historian with a particular interest in the community in which we lived. Rather than teaching history out of a book, Adam had a strong commitment to bringing history to life through the folks who had lived it. At the time, this kind of "oral history" was still new, and Adam had done a good job of promoting it to the community and the university's administration.

During several of our chats over coffee, Adam related his personal experience with psychotherapy. As a graduate student, Adam had suffered from a monumental writer's block. He was 3 years into graduate school, and was under pressure to write his dissertation. For reasons he didn't understand, he hadn't been able to produce even the first word of the first paragraph of the first page. He clearly loved his field, and he knew that by not writing his dissertation he was jeopardizing his chances for a satisfying career.

He finally discussed his anxiety and growing fear with his faculty advisor, who then referred him to a well-respected psychoanalyst, Dr. Roberts, who taught at the university. When Adam first met with Dr.

Roberts, the doctor sported a beautiful Scottish tweed jacket and had a goatee. His large office was decorated with impressive artwork and many diplomas and certificates. His private practice was extensive, unusual in a university setting. He had published widely, and had been successful as a professor and as a training analyst. For Adam, Dr. Roberts exemplified a successful academic and professional.

Adam saw Dr. Roberts regularly for 18 months. They were making wonderful progress. Adam's self-esteem was blossoming. His relationship with women had never been better. He was getting along well with his friends and his family. Dr. Roberts told Adam's faculty advisor that Adam had made significant emotional headway. But he still had not written the first word of his dissertation. His faculty advisor was concerned because time was running out, and Adam's doctorate was at stake. At his faculty advisor's suggestion, Adam discontinued psychoanalysis with Dr. Roberts and began treatment with a research psychologist at the university. Dr. Markson was a world-renowned experimental psychologist whose specialty was animal behavior. Under ordinary circumstances, he did not see, let alone treat, people.

Adam described his first meeting with Dr. Markson. "I stood outside the door of the research lab, knocked politely, and waited. The 'No Admittance' sign seemed to specifically be for me." Finally, about 5 minutes after the appointment time, Markson emerged from his lab. "When he came bursting out," Adam continued, "he looked at me as if I were one of his misbehaving rats; he obviously resented the interruption."

Adam began to tell Dr. Markson his tale of woe: the unwritten dissertation, his advisor's concern, and his anxiety that he was rapidly reaching a dead end in his chances for an academic career. The researcher waved his hand at Adam as if he were swatting a fly.

"Understand," he said, wagging a dirty finger at Adam, "I am meeting with you only because I owe your faculty advisor a big favor." He handed Adam a crumpled paper, and said, "Read this, sign it, and come next Monday at 8 a.m. with your checkbook." With that, he turned his back and disappeared into the sanctuary of his lab. Adam noted dryly, "Instead of the 50-minute hour, I got the 2-minute drill."

Adam walked to his car and got in before he unfolded the crumpled paper. It was a contract, and as he told me about this experience, he pulled out a copy of the contract, now wrinkled and yellow with age. Here's what it said:

> You [name here], agree to the following:
>
> Initially, you will write three checks of $100 each to three charities of your choice.
>
> 1. You are to bring to my office every Monday morning by 10 a.m. 10 typed pages of your dissertation. I may or may not read them.

I am not your advisor or editor. All I expect is 10 typewritten pages that have something to do with your dissertation.

2. If by 10 a.m. each Monday your 10 typewritten pages are not under my door, one of those checks will be mailed. No excuses of any kind will be accepted or wanted. You or your family could be hospitalized, incapacitated, etc. It won't matter. No excuses of any kind. It's 10 pages and if they aren't delivered, you've contributed $100 to charity.
3. If all three checks have been forfeited, then this contract is over and I will call your advisor and tell him that one, you're a loser, two, I don't want to be bothered with any of your drivel any more, and three, he owes me.
4. This contract will begin when you sign it and return it to me. Don't bother me under any circumstances. I am not interested in your questions or concerns. If you really must know, I've already wasted too much time on you.

As Adam showed me the faded contract, he said, "I've always kept this because it reminds me of how close I came to losing my career. It makes me realize that if I ever need a kick in the rear, I know exactly where to go to get it." But the story doesn't end there.

"I picked three charities," Adam went on, "the ACLU, the Red Cross, and the Salvation Army. I figured that if I did tank, at least the money would go to a good cause. And," he said, remembering the contract, "that was a lot of money to me. I had just a few hundred dollars in savings and my stipend to get me through the semester."

Adam continued, "I signed the checks and the contract with a heavy heart; I had a question that would go unanswered: Where was therapy's "unconditional positive regard" when I needed it? On Monday morning, I slid the packet of stuff under the professor's laboratory door and went home to sit at my typewriter. I knew one thing, and that was that I could crank out ten pages in an hour or two, so my $300 was going to be safe."

"I banged out the 10 pages angrily, keeping my pledge for the first week. After a year and a half of not being able to write anything, my frustration and anger kicked in, and I couldn't wait to get those pages written and shoved under his damned door. Besides, I didn't care what I wrote; I just wanted this guy off my back. He was a jerk who had already decided that I was a loser. Writing the 10 pages was surprisingly easy!"

When Adam looked at those 10 pages later, he realized he was actually well on his way. He continued to write 10 pages a week. He couldn't believe how easy it was to get those 10 pages under Markson's door each Monday.

Six months later, he was still writing. "In my opinion," Adam said, smiling, "some of it was pretty good. But then I got overconfident and began to procrastinate, not writing anything until Saturday morning, then Sunday morning, then Sunday night." After 4 weeks of this, Adam realized he was in trouble. He called Dr. Markson and explained to his secretary that he was having difficulty writing again. The secretary called him back and gave him an appointment, crisply informing him that he had 15 minutes, no more.

"I thought," Adam said ruefully, "I'd be able to renegotiate the contract. Boy, was I kidding myself about that." Dr. Markson was cold, displeased, and thoroughly uninterested in Adam's difficulties. Adam tried to explain how he was struggling, and said that he thought he could live with donating $100 to the ACLU. Markson muttered, "Unacceptable."

Adam recounted, "Then he looked at me with disgust, and directed me to return at the same time the next day. I walked out, thoroughly convinced that I was going to get tossed out of my program and lose my teaching assistantship."

"The next morning, Dr. Markson handed me the three checks I'd written, and said, 'Tear them up and write three new checks—each for $150, and made out to the Ku Klux Klan of Louisiana, the American Nazi Party, and the National Rifle Association. Slide them under the door with the rest of your stuff. You can go now.'"

Adam went on. "I realized sometime later that he must have gone to the trouble of calling my advisor, because he had selected the three most loathsome organizations I could have thought of." Adam was genuinely surprised that the professor had gone to that kind of trouble.

"After that, I left his office. I was so mad that I again began to write, furious, saying to myself, 'the hell with Markson.' And, I continued to write until I was done."

Six months later, Adam turned in his dissertation. After it was accepted he got a call from Markson's secretary. "She had an envelope for me, and when I went to pick it up, it had the title 'Adam's Trash' on the front. In it were my three checks and not another damned thing. No message, no congratulations, but I did have my checks back. I wrote, 'Null and Void' on each one, and I saved them. I still have those checks. Over the years when I have felt my writer's block returning, I get those checks and the contract out. Just looking at them somehow breaks down the block. As a matter of fact, I looked at them yesterday, and suddenly getting my grades done and turned in didn't seem so daunting!"

We laughed and finished our coffee. When I next saw Adam, he told me that those three magical checks were still operational. He had gotten his tests graded and turned in that morning.

As Adam told his story, I started to wonder about the therapeutic relationship. At least in this case, the gentle, empathic therapist had failed to start Adam writing, while the researcher's demanding and unsupportive approach was powerfully effective in getting Adam past a monumental writer's block.

We assume that a warm, positive relationship between psychotherapist and client is a crucial factor for successful therapy. Adam's case suggests that this may not always be as important as we have assumed. The emotional comfort Adam gained from Dr. Roberts did not help him write his dissertation. Rather, Dr. Markson's operant conditioning model, with a significantly negative reinforcement, the loss of big bucks and a career, was the motivator and the key to Adam's later success.

Adam's case may have been exceptional. But there is nothing that says we can't learn something about psychotherapy from a single case. Moreover, it illuminates the point that motivation and measurable goals may be more important to the success of psychotherapy than the emotional relationship of client and psychotherapist.

Case 48: Joseph

The case of Joseph, a diagnosed criminal psychopath who was a sex offender, provides another example of behavior conditioning as a form of psychotherapy. A lean, tattooed 20-year-old man, he had spent most of his adolescence in juvenile detention for one offense or another, and had finally been convicted of forcing an 8-year-old boy to perform sexual acts. He was committed to a mental hospital. At that time, our state hospitals had a number of cases like this, and were mandated by law to provide appropriate psychotherapy for the patients.

I was reluctant to treat Joseph, knowing that therapeutic efforts with sex offenders are seldom successful and have a high recidivism rate. In a Canadian study, the authors estimate that 37% of sex offenders will return to the correctional system (Langevin et al., 2004), but I owed the superintendent a favor. So I agreed to treat him. Joseph was cooperative and understood why we were treating him, but he was mostly motivated by the opportunity to see what he could learn through psychotherapy about additional ways to manipulate others.

I developed a behavior-conditioning program for Joseph. First, I assembled a set of pictures of children at play that I had clipped from magazines and newspapers. I hooked Joseph to biofeedback equipment to measure his emotional and physical responses. They included heart rate, muscle tension, and sweat gland activity, all indicators of sexual arousal. I explained to him that I would show him these pictures one by one and that every time the equipment indicated a physical or emotional response, he would get a negative reinforcement. I had several vials of chemicals with noxious fumes—ammonia, bleach, vomit, and feces. Each time Joseph responded to a picture, I'd have him take a sniff of one of the vials and snap a rubber band on his wrist.

None of these negative reinforcements was overpowering or painful, but they *were* negative. After 2½ months, our thrice-weekly sessions began showing results. None of the measurements were indicating any particular responsiveness, and I felt that we were making some progress.

Joseph's psychiatrist, having read the case notes that showed "slight improvement," granted Joseph a 4-hour pass to go to the library. Watched by the library security guards, Joseph was interrupted as he followed a young girl into the ladies room. He was arrested and sentenced to a long term in the state penitentiary. It was not possible to know whether the treatment would have worked with time, but my efforts and Joseph's responses did provide a benchmark and a series of measurements.

Today, the equipment and method would be far more sophisticated, and would have measured pupil dilation or perhaps blood circulation in specific areas of the brain. And, in the years that have passed, literature and research have confirmed that biofeedback can be effective if administered effectively and in a timely manner. In 2010 alone, researchers demonstrated that biofeedback for heart rate variability (Wheat et al., 2010), irritable bowel syndrome (Shinozaki et al., 2010) chronic low back pain (Kapitza et al. 2010), and decubitus ulcers were all conditions that could be eased with biofeedback. Secondary outcomes for the studies included improvements in emotional health, depression, and improvement in psychopathologies.

Case 49: Jane and Jill

An interesting example of a scientific advance in psychotherapy is eye movement desensitization and reprocessing (EMDR), developed in the late 1980s by the psychologist Francine Shapiro. I used this method with two sisters, Jane and Jill, ages 12 and 10, who were referred to me by their family physician. They had suffered stress and smoke inhalation as a result of a fire in the family home. While EMDR was a fairly new psychotherapy at that time, there was emerging research evidence that it was effective in treating trauma and stress disorders. More recent writing, edited by Shapiro and now in its third printing, demonstrates the efficacy of EMDR across a number of treatment orientations (Shapiro, 2002).

A month before I met them, the girls had been celebrating Halloween, when a candle fell onto a paper and set fire to the curtains. The house was small and quickly filled with smoke. Their father came into the room, grabbed the fire extinguisher from the kitchen, and quickly put out the fire. Both girls had inhaled smoke, and were traumatized by the fire, and the danger and chaos of the event.

Their parents took them to the emergency room, where they were given oxygen and inhalants. Over the next few weeks both girls had nightmares and would wake up screaming. Both were anxious all the time. The 10-year-old, Jill, burst into tears at the least provocation.

Their doctor had treated them with antidepressants, but the parents were reluctant to medicate their daughters and looked for an alternative way to deal with their stress and anxiety. The pediatrician thought a few sessions with me might help prevent the girls' symptoms from escalating into full-blown post-traumatic stress disorder.

I had attended a workshop on EMDR for children, and I thought it might be a fast, nonthreatening solution, particularly since its effectiveness was supported by some fairly impressive scientific evidence. During EMDR treatments, the therapist moves his finger back and forth in front of the client's eyes, asking the client to follow the finger with his or her eyes, but without turning the head. While no one is exactly sure how or why the treatment works, research demonstrates that many people show a significant measurable improvement in symptoms like nightmares, which are common in post-traumatic stress disorder. The reasoning behind EMDR is that as the client's eyes shift back and forth, opposite sides of the brain are activated. This appears to cause changes in emotional reactivity.

I explained my plan to the girls' parents, who agreed to the treatment, provided it would help quickly and not frighten the girls. I said that I would willingly use EMDR on my own daughters, and that seemed to reassure them.

First, I explained to the girls that I thought their anxiety and nightmares were a result of their experience with the fire. I told them that I would have to ask them to remember the fire again, and that this might be frightening, but that they could ask me to stop at any time if they became too scared, just by holding their hand up in a "Stop" gesture. I also explained that what I was going to do with them helped people who were having nightmares. With some apprehension they agreed to the treatment.

I began the session by recounting an anecdote from my own family. When my own children were small, we had had not one, but two fires at our house, a few months apart. My wife and I woke, saw flames, called the Fire Department, and were outside when the firemen came. By the time the fire department came the second time, one of my daughters, who was 4 at the time, said, "Fires aren't so bad once you get used to them!" This anecdote relaxed the sisters and reassured them that others had been through fires and had been okay afterwards.

I taught the girls a breathing exercise that would help them calm down if they became anxious during the treatment. I then had them both imagine the fire again, and then measured their anxiety after the description with a test called the Subjective Units of Disturbance Scale (SUDS). SUDS is a commonly used psychological measurement tool that measures tension and fear on a 10-point scale, with 10 being the highest amount of fear and tension. Both girls measured at about 9, meaning they were still quite fearful.

After measuring their disturbance at this negative image, I suggested a positive thought: "I am no longer in danger." Then I used another measurement, the Validity of Cognition Scale (VOC), which measures the believability of a statement on a scale of 1 to 7, with 1 meaning that they do not believe the statement at all, and 7 meaning that they believe it to be completely true. Jane scored a 2 and Jill a 1, indicating that they still believed themselves to be in danger.

Asking the girls to think about the worst picture and a best, happy picture without the fire, I then began the eye movement procedure. They were eventually able to follow my finger with just their eyes as they switched from the memory of the fire to feelings of being safe.

After the sixth treatment session, I stopped to reevaluate. Jane's SUDS measurement had dropped to 5.5, but Jill's anxiety was measured at a 9. She reported some feelings of tension and anxiety about the procedure itself, saying it "made her nervous." So I began seeing the sisters separately. I used a more standard desensitization program for Jill, which included guided imagery and diaphragmatic breathing.

In another month, the SUDS measurements had dropped considerably for both girls. Jane's measured at 2.0, and Jill had a measurement of 2.9. In follow-up sessions 2 and then 6 months later, the measurements were slightly lower, and the girls were recovering.

This case demonstrates that an approach that succeeds with one client may not work with another, even though the symptoms, and in this case, the root cause, are very similar. Psychologically, one size treatment does not fit all. For me, the case also illustrates the importance of frequent measures of progress in psychotherapy. As I analyzed the results midway through treatment, I was able to adjust it in ways that best suited my two young clients.

EMDR is just one example of psychotherapy becoming more science-based. Let me briefly review a few more psychotherapy concepts that are supported by research.

Operant conditioning was first utilized and popularized by B.F. Skinner (Skinner, 1930). He and others who followed demonstrated that a very powerful way to change behavior was to apply different reinforcement schedules. Although Skinner was primarily a research psychologist and most of his work involved the conditioning of animals, he nevertheless saw operant conditioning as an approach with possibilities for human behavior; he even described a therapeutic community that practiced operant conditioning principles for its members.

Here's an example of operant conditioning that anyone can relate to. Think about sitting in front of a machine with lots of blinking lights and exciting sounds. You push a button to activate it. Sometimes it pays you a lot, and sometimes it pays you a little. Sometimes it rewards you with an enormous sum of money, and the bells ring and lights flash. It's a slot machine!

In much the same way, reinforcement procedures can work in psychotherapy. In the case of the encopretic boy I described in Chapter 5, "The Psychotherapist as Artist," part of the treatment was having him clean himself up and do his own laundry. Negative reinforcement seems like a reasonable thing to do, and it *does* discourage bad behavior. As with Adam, our college professor, even the threat of negative reinforcement can be a powerful deterrent. And think about every time you stop at a stop sign. You know what might happen if you don't—a ticket, an accident, or worse. All these are negative reinforcements.

Operant conditioning is not limited to negative reinforcement. Positive reinforcement—praise, complements, affection—goes clearly back to the reinforcement theories of Pavlov and his salivating dogs. Pavlov performed the early work on classical conditioning in the 1890s. A physiologist and physician who was investigating the digestive process, he would ring a bell, and the dogs he used as subjects would get food, stimulating the flow of their saliva. What Pavlov discovered was that after a certain number of presentations of the bell and food, the saliva would flow at just the sound of the bell. The dogs had been conditioned. This was an early example of what is known as classical learning. In classical learning, you first present the stimulus, the bell, and then the reinforcement, the food.

In the late 1930s, and into the 1940s and 1950s, B. F. Skinner continued to explore the conditioning process through his work as a research psychologist. His subjects, unlike Pavlov's, had to actually do something to receive an award; hence, he used the word *operant*. Skinner also pointed out the effects of two schedules of reinforcement: interval, meaning how much time elapses between reinforcement, and ratio, meaning how many responses the subject has to make before they can receive the reward. Skinner found that by varying these two components, he could build very strong response programs that were very resistant to extinction, meaning that the individual would continue to respond, even for long periods of time between reinforcements. To go back to our example of the slot machine earlier in this chapter, if a slot machine only delivers a reward some of the time, on what psychologists call a "variable schedule," it's a way of building a persistent behavior.

A method of psychotherapy that evolved from operant conditioning is called systematic desensitization. This approach trains clients to systematically overcome phobias through progressive exposure; it is the treatment of choice, based on solid research, for phobias.

If you recall the young man who was discussed in Chapter 1 who could not go to fast food restaurants with his friends, you'll know that by slowly reintroducing the components of eating out, such as walking by a restaurant, entering it and leaving, and finally staying for a meal, are examples of systematic desensitization.

Case 50: Billy

Another example of systematic desensitization is found in the following case of a boy who was terrified of water. Marianne brought her 10-year-old son, Billy, to see me because he was deathly afraid of water and terrified of learning how to swim. I developed a plan for Marianne to follow, because I wanted to involve her. It is my experience in treating phobic children that they have probably picked up their fear from someone in the family. In Billy's case, Marianne demonstrated concern—no, fear—when her son was in situations that she was unfamiliar with or couldn't control. While she presented Billy as the fearful one, I thought that her own fear was a factor. Her fear became his phobia. I needed to reassure her that he would be safe during the systematic desensitization.

First, I had her take Billy to the local YMCA and simply show him the 3½-foot pool through the observation window. The second step was to have him enter the room where the pool was, and stay only until he became uneasy, even if it were only a minute or two. In Step 3 Billy would sit on the bleachers in the pool room, again for only as long as it took him to become anxious. After each pool encounter, Marianne was to reward him with a small candy bar from the vending machine. As Marianne rewarded Billy, she was also rewarding herself for Billy's safety.

For the next step Billy was to sit at the edge of the pool. Again, he was to stay only as long as he could without becoming anxious, and once again he would be rewarded with a candy bar. He then dangled one foot, only to the ankle, into the water, and then both feet, in the part of the pool with steps. Finally, he was to stand briefly in the pool. Eventually Billy was able to lower himself in the pool, and finally, able to put his face in the water. Before long, he was swimming and both he and his mother had reduced their fear of water.

It's important to note that as clients learn the techniques of systematic desensitization, they are also developing a tool for treating themselves in other fearful circumstances, and perhaps reducing the possibility of developing phobias in the first place.

Another application of scientific principles to psychotherapy is with the concept of flow, developd by Mihály Csíkszentmihályi (1990), a psychologist and anthropologist who was affiliated with University of Chicago. Flow describes a psychological state of energized focus and near-full involvement. It is characterized by clear goals, regular feedback, and deep immersion in a task or activity that is neither too difficult nor too easy, but rather "optimally challenging" (p. 209). Often a person in a state of flow will lose track of time during the activity. Csíkszentmihályi's research in the 1970s, on which his theory of flow is based, used his experience sampling method. In his research, respondents wore a pager. The pager was randomly set during the day, and when the subject was paged, they were instructed to respond to a questionnaire. In addition to establishing their whereabouts, current mental and emotional states, and level of self-esteem, the questionnaire also asked them to measure the level of challenge and the skill they had to meet the challenge. Both were measured on a scale of 1 (low) to 10 (high).

Csíkszentmihályi established that the higher the levels of perceived challenge and skill, the higher the likelihood that the subject was in a state of flow. He also observed that when individuals were in flow, they were often unaware of time passing. In his book *The Evolving Self*, published in 1993, Csíkszentmihályi points out, "People who are often in Flow have higher self-esteem than those who experience Flow rarely. Teenagers who report more Flow tend to be happier and they develop academic talents further than teens who are in Flow less often. Adults who spend more time in Flow work longer, yet are less prone to work-related illnesses." He notes that "Individuals who cannot experience Flow or who enjoy only passive and simple activities end up developing selves that are often in turmoil, driven by frustration and disappointment" (p. 204).

Csíkszentmihályi's work suggests that psychotherapists would do well to find ways to encourage their clients to experience flow. Flow training might be considered one of the new roles of the research psychologist as psychotherapist.

One of the significant advances in psychotherapy since Freud was generated by Aaron Beck (1967, 1976). Conducting research in the areas of psychotherapy, psychopathology, suicide, and psychometrics, Beck, a psychiatrist, studied depression extensively and then developed scales to measure the extent of the client's depression, hopelessness, and possibility of suicide (Beck, Ward, Mendelson, Mock, & Erbaugh 1961). These scales are still used widely today by clinicians to determine the intensity of clients' depression. The school of cognitive behavior therapy outlined a technique for modifying depression by changing the client's thinking and feeling about what he or she was experiencing. This proved to be a research-proven method of treating depression.

Cognitive behavior therapy (CBT) is a psychotherapeutic approach that uses a goal-oriented, systematic procedure to help clients address unhealthy emotions, behaviors, and thoughts. CBT has demonstrated effectiveness for a number of problems, including mood disorders, anxiety, personality and eating, disorder, substance abuse, and psychoses. Treatment is often directed at specific identified psychological problems and is time-limited.

The concept of helplessness as the foundation for much of depression has been especially important in the shift toward positive psychology. Seligman's work (1998, 2002) and additional research done in cognitive behavior therapy suggest that when clients can challenge their negative thoughts, the intensity of the thoughts will often be reduced. Individuals who are resilient and have lives filled with experiences that give them a feeling of mastery and control usually experience measurably less depression, tension, and anxiety.

When psychotherapists focus on these positive and preventive principles, they can help clients recognize that they can take control of their lives, that they need not feel helpless in the face of adversity or emotional distress. This feeling of mastery builds optimism and guards against depression—and can be a basic construct of living a more successful and positive life.

Taking Seligman's ideas a step further is research by Rebecca Logsdon and Linda Teri, which showed that simply "pleasant events," bingo, for example, could reduce depression in nursing home patients. Activity therapists have known this for years. Logsdon and Teri's work included developing a measurable Pleasant Events Schedule (1997), with a list of activities that could be used to activate lethargic or depressed nursing home patients. Their work has given psychotherapists an opportunity to consider activities beyond standard psychotherapy as part of their therapeutic toolboxes. There are follow-up studies underway to determine if utilizing the Pleasant Events Schedule can be used as a preventive measure.

Clinical practice and research is still another piece of the ever-expanding psychotherapy treatment puzzle. In the article "Clinical Practice as Natural Laboratory for Psychotherapy Research," by Jeffrey Borckardt and his colleagues, published in the *American Psychologist* in 2008, the authors suggest that clinical practice itself should serve as a laboratory and those psychotherapists should actually systematically measure and regularly report patient progress. The authors also point out that frequent assessments during psychotherapy would produce an enormous amount of useful research data. This data could help guide the practice of psychotherapy now and in the future.

I believe that this kind of research and therapeutic accountability will change the way psychotherapy is practiced. Treatment progress will be evidence-based. Goals will be set clearly and early in the process. Evaluation will take place frequently. Ideally, this approach will be both therapeutic and preventive, and in my judgment will broaden the definition of psychotherapy, much as the work of Logsdon and Teri did with their Pleasant Events Schedule work.

The work of the psychotherapist as research psychologist can and should provide new roles for the psychotherapist that can and will be used to benefit psychotherapy clients in both treatment and prevention.

Conclusion

A New World of Psychotherapy

In a 2011 paper by Alan Kazdin and Stacey Blasé, in *Perspectives in Psychological Science*, the authors state, "at any given time approximately 70% of the individuals in need of psychological services do not receive them." According to Kazdin and Blasé, "While one-on-one psychotherapy will always have a valued place, the discipline needs to supplement it with an entire portfolio of new models for delivering interventions focused on both prevention and treatment of mental and substance abuse disorders." They continue, "Possibilities include the use of media, self-help approaches, technology, lay people and new settings for interventions" (Kazdin & Blasé, 2011, pp. 21–37).

I agree with Kazdin's and Blasé's views, which are also supported by the New York State Psychological Association's (NYSPA) think tank presentation in 2011, which I described in Chapter 12. The acceptance and use of the roles I have suggested, along with new psychotherapy models and delivery systems, will define the practices of the future. For example, the psychotherapist as navigator makes a strong case for measuring client strengths and weaknesses before beginning psychotherapy, and routinely assessing progress as a central element of psychotherapy. Without this kind of rigor, psychotherapy is in danger of "drifting," at great cost to clients and providers.

Psychotherapy as a field has already made significant progress. The range of services currently offered—including cognitive behavioral therapy, social skills training, and other well-tested modalities—is remarkable. Still, more change is needed, and I am optimistic that the advancements that lie ahead will be profound, and will mandate that psychotherapists choose from an ever-broader modality of treatment approaches and an expanded choice of roles.

One of the barriers to advancement is whether the cost of recordkeeping, services, and training will be astronomical. That is very likely. But consider the other side of this particular coin: the significant drain on the economy caused by untreated or undertreated mental disorders. For example, the national cost of depression is estimated at $40 billion a year. Will the savings that can result from working "smarter"—as I've suggested throughout this book—offset the additional costs for more services? I believe it will. Services that are improved and processes that are streamlined will offset the cost of the fears, anxieties, and phobias psychotherapists treat. The costs of client pain, both for individuals and for our culture, are huge.

The roles in this book are only a sample of the many roles psychotherapists may be able to apply to their work with clients, but all offer clear examples of the value of emerging roles.

The psychotherapist as navigator presents a clear picture of using mapping and charting to measure improvement against set goals, providing evidence for the value of practice and justifying its cost in an environment of rising costs.

The psychotherapist as coach promotes emotional strength training, which has been shown to prevent psychological damage and head off future trauma. The role of psychotherapist as conservationist offers an opportunity to move psychotherapy toward preventative mental health practices. Prevention, in the long run, almost always generates significant savings financially, and preserves personal energy. Such practices allow psychotherapists to work with clients in the interests of emotional and mental sustainability. Autogenic training, conflict resolution, and creative ways of problem-solving all reduce stress, enhance resilience, and build optimism. The psychotherapist as researcher is a role that could be adapted from the field of public health. Participatory research programs in public health demonstrate a crossroad between science and outreach. In efforts to address community issues such as bullying, community divisiveness, pervasive poverty, and drug addiction, scientists share their findings with the "feet on the street"—police forces, fire departments, school personnel, and first responders.

The choice of roles for psychotherapists gives opportunities to model psychotherapy on proven practices in other fields. While it is understandable for psychotherapy to embrace practices from its own field, an expansion to adapt best practices from other fields opens up opportunities for psychotherapists and their clients.

In addition to concerns about cost-cutting, psychotherapy as a field must continually acknowledge and honor the human trait of resistance to change. This may be particularly true of those who are motivated or mandated to seek psychotherapy. It is this very resistance to change that can be treated through an abundance of roles that the psychotherapist can choose from. The right role, used with the right client, creates a safe environment for clients to learn how to change unproductive behaviors. Think back to Case 3, in Chapter 1, where the role of coach created common ground for a battling couple. Or think of the psychotherapist as music teacher, where practice is used to overcome resistance. Practice does not always mean perfect, but it generally creates familiarity and its accompanying comfort.

Most importantly, the adaptation of new roles for psychotherapists that I propose in this book will increase the effectiveness of psychotherapy and improve client outcomes. The psychotherapist who functions as a music teacher can go beyond the 50-minute hour by offering clients home practice assignments. The psychotherapist as advertising executive has the unique ability to expand therapeutic goals by helping clients rebrand themselves. The psychotherapist as artist can present new perspectives that lead to powerful changes in how clients view their worlds. The psychotherapist as editor guides clients to new narratives that will change their view of themselves.

Case 1 in Chapter 1 of this book, about Margaret and her high-risk pregnancy, demonstrates more than any case I can think of the importance of being flexible as a therapist. As you will recall, hypnotic treatment helped her maintain a pregnancy after a threatened miscarriage.

I go back to Margaret as a humbling reminder to myself. My goal with her was to assure that she did not lose her baby. While we succeeded in meeting that immediate and critical goal, I considered my work with Margaret completed. But, as the old saying goes, it ain't over 'til the fat lady sings, or in this case, delivers. I didn't think through to the obvious conclusion—that at some point she was going to have to deliver that baby. It was this oversight on my part that led a surprising phone call from Margaret 6 months later. I was excited, thinking she had delivered and was calling me with good news. But the minute I heard her soft voice on the phone I knew something was wrong

"How are you doing?" I asked.

"Well, everything was going great," she said, "but now there's a terrible problem. I was due to deliver last week, had contractions, but nothing happened, so they sent me home. Yesterday, the same thing—I stayed in the hospital for 4 hours, and still nothing. Efforts to induce were not successful, so the doctor wants to go ahead and do a cesarean, but I don't want to do that, so I'm calling you for help."

It was at that minute that I realized with a shock that I had given Margaret repeated—and I do mean repeated—hypnotic suggestions to hold onto the baby and keep it safe inside. At the time, I hadn't even considered giving her suggestions to deliver. I was so focused on the challenge of helping her keep her baby that I that I hadn't even thought of her delivering. By then my wife had delivered five children. I took delivery for granted.

Switching gears immediately, I urged Margaret to come to my office immediately so that we could remove the hypnotic suggestion that was preventing her from delivering. Panicked now, she told me that her doctor wouldn't let her drive the 30 miles to my office this close to delivery. I made plans to drive to her house that evening, after my last client. I'd be there about 6:00 p.m., I said. She began to cry, and begged me to hypnotize her over the phone immediately.

I can't tell you the level of misgiving I had. In order to guide a client into a trance, at least for me, it's important to be able to watch the progress—for instance, monitoring the person's breathing or whether their eyelids become heavy when I suggest that. But because Margaret sounded desperate, I decided to go ahead with phone hypnosis.

I waited on the phone while she got comfortable in her bedroom and lay down with pillows all around her, the speaker phone beside her. I told her to start relaxing very deeply and to breathe slowly and comfortably. After that, I asked her to remember what she did when we worked together earlier, and to remember it so well that she could now find herself going comfortably and easily into a hypnotic state.

For the next 45 minutes I conducted a phone hypnosis in which I first removed all my previous injunctions to hold and retain the baby she was carrying, and then to begin to relax and push ever so gently. I also reminded her of the book we had used in our sessions together, *The Lost Princess of Oz*. She was particularly fond of the ending of the book where the Wizard pries open the two halves of the golden peach shell with a knife, and lo and behold, the lost fairy princess emerges:

> As the two halves fell apart, a pink, cloud-like haze came pouring from the golden peach-pit, almost filling the big room, and from the haze a form took shape and settled beside them. Then, as the haze faded away, a sweet voice said, "Thank you, my friends!" and before them stood their lovely girl Ruler, Ozma of Oz.
>
> (Baum, 1917, p. 298)

For Margaret, this was a joyous event at the end of the book. Margaret was in a fairly deep state of hypnosis, so I gave her an injunction to have a quick and relatively pain-free delivery. I told her to come out of the trance. She did so, saying that she was really excited and felt great. She was headed to the hospital, she said, for "an easy delivery."

I asked her to have her husband, Doug, call me when she delivered. I got the call at 4:30 the next morning, and he said that both he and Margaret were happy and appreciative. I was just relieved. I talked to her the next day and she told me it went so well even the doctor was surprised. She thanked me and said she was very grateful. I was grateful too. She sent me a picture of the baby, a darling little boy, at 3 months, and I was quite the proud therapist, feeling that I had had a part in bringing him into the world.

The story of Margaret demonstrates once again the importance of adaptation in psychotherapeutic practice. Not only did I have to gain a new perspective and set new goals for treatment, I had to work under less than ideal circumstances. I had to use what was then considered the newest technology—a speaker phone—to deliver services to a client. I also had to venture into new territory with no real preparation or training in teletherapy, now quite common.

For the psychotherapist, new roles, adaptation, provide the best lessons of all: those learned from clients themselves. In shaping this new world of psychotherapy, therapists will themselves experience over and over the exhilaration and excitement that comes with change.

Bibliography

Academy of Cognitive Therapy. (n.d.). http://www.academyofct.org./library.

Adams, J. (1980). *Conceptual blockbusting* (2nd ed.). New York: Norton.

Baum, L. F. (1917). *The lost princess of Oz*. Chicago, IL: Reilly & Britton.

Beck, A. T. (1967). *Depression: Clinical, experimental and theoretical aspects*. New York: Hoeber.

Beck, A. T. (1976). *Cognitive therapy and the emotional disorders*. New York: Meridian.

Beck A. T., Ward C. H., Mendelson, M., Mock, J., & Erbaugh, J. (1961, June). An inventory for measuring depression. *Archives of General Psychiatry, 4*(6), 561–571. doi:10.1001/archpsyc.1961.01710120031004. PMID 13688369.

Berkman, L. F., & Syme, S. L. (1979). Social networks, host resistance and mortality: A nine-year followup study of Alameda County residents. *American Journal of Epidemiology, 109*, 186–204.

Berne, E. (1964). *Games people play*. New York: Grove Press.

Borckardt, J. J., Nash, M. R., Murphy, M. D., Moore, M., Shaw, D., & O'Neil, P. (2008, February-March). Clinical practice as natural laboratory for psychotherapy research. *American Psychologist, 63*(2), 77–95.

Bruner, J. (1990) *Acts of meaning*. Cambridge, MA: Harvard University Press.

Carr, A. (2004). *Positive psychology: The science of happiness and human strengths*. New York: Brunner-Routledge.

Catell, A., Catell, K., & Catell, H. (1993). *16PF Questionnaire* (5th ed.). Champaign, IL: Institute for Personality and Ability Testing, Inc.

Cherepov, G. (1971). *Discovering oil painting*. New York: Watson-Guptill.

Chronical of Guidance Publications: Chemical Engineer. (2003). Moravia, New York: Author.

Coliccio, T. (2000). *Think like a chef*. New York: Random House.

Costello, L. B., & Reich, R. (2009). *Notes on cooking: A short guide to an essential craft*. New York: RCR Creative Press.

Csíkzentmahályi, M. (1990). *Flow: The psychology of optimal experience*. New York: HarperCollins.

Csíkzentmahályi, M. (1993). *The evolving self*. New York: HarperCollins.

deBono, E. (1970). *deBono's training course*. New York: Facts on File.

deShazer, S. (1985). *Keys to solution in brief therapy*. New York. Norton.

Dobson, D., & Dobson, K. (2009). *Evidence-based practice of cognitive-behavioral therapy*. New York Guilford.

Epston, D., & White, M. (1992). *Experience, contradiction, narrative and imagination: Selected papers of David Epston and Michael White, 1989–1991.* South Australia: Dulwich Centre Publications.

Gendlin, E. (1978). *Focusing.* New York: Everest House.

Gottman, J. (1999). *The marriage clinic: A scientifically-based marital therapy.* New York: Norton.

Gottman, J., & Silver, N. (1999). *The seven principles for making marriage work.* New York: Crown.

Haley, J. (1999). *Uncommon therapy: The psychiatric techniques of Milton H. Erickson, M.D.* New York: Norton. (Original work published 1973)

Haley, J. (1976). *Problem solving therapy.* San Francisco: Jossey-Bass.

Harris, T. (1964). *I'm ok—you're ok.* New York: Harper & Row.

Herk, N., & Thompson, R. (2012). Strong Interest Inventory [Manual supplement]. Occupational scales update. Mountain View, CA: CCP.

Kahneman, D. (2011). *Thinking, fast and slow.* New York: Farrar, Straus & Giroux.

Kapitza, K. P., Passie, T., Bernateck, M., & Karst, M. (2010) First non-contingent respiratory biofeedback placebo versus contingent biofeedback in patients with chronic low back pain: A randomized, controlled double-blind trial. *Applied Psychophysiology and Biofeedback, 35*(3) 207–217.

Karpman, S. (1968, April). Fairytales and script drama analysis. *Transactional Analysis Bulletin, 7*(26), 39–43.

Kazdin, A., & Blasé, S. (2011). Rebooting psychotherapy research and practice to reduce the burden of mental illness. *Perspectives in Psychological Science, (Series) Monitor on Psychology, 6*(1), 21–37.

Koberg, D., & Bagnall, J. (2003). *The revised, all-new universal traveler: A soft systems guide to creativity, problem-solving, and the process of seeking goals.* Los Altos, CA: Crisp.

L'Abate, L. (2009). The drama triangle: Therapy, theory and practice. *American Journal of Family Therapy, 37,* 1–11.

Langevin, R., Curnoe, S., Fedoroff, P., Bennett, R., Langevin, M., Peever, C., ... Sandhu, S. (2004, October). Lifetime sex offender recidivism: A 25-year follow-up study. *Canadian Journal of Criminology and Criminal Justice,* 532–550.

Lahner, J. (2007). *Proust was a neuroscientist.* New York: Houghton Mifflin.

Leising, D. (2008). Applying principles of intercultural communication to personality disorder therapy. *Psychology and Psychotherapy, 81,* 261–272.

Lingelbach, J., & Purcell, L. (Eds.). (2000). *Hands-on nature.* Woodstock, VT: Vermont Institute of Natural History. (Original work published 1986)

Logsdon, R. G., & Teri, L. (1997). Pleasant Events Schedule-AD: Psychometric properties and relationship to depression and cognition in Alzheimer disease patients. *The Gerontologist, 37*(1), 40–45.

Luborsky, L. (1962). Clinicians' judgment of mental health: A proposed scale. *Archives of General Psychiatry, 7,* 407–417.

Luborsky, L., Chandler, M., Auerbach, A. H., Cohen, J., & Bachrach, H. M. (1972). Factors influencing the outcome of psychotherapy: A review of quantitative research. *Psychological Bulletin, 75,* 145–185.

Madanes, C. (1990). *Sex, love and violence: Strategies for transformation.* New York: Norton.

Masters, W. H., & Johnson, V. E. (1970). *Human sexual inadequacy.* Boston, MA: Little, Brown.
Meeks, S., Shah, S. N., & Ramsey, S. K. (2009). The Pleasant Events Scale—Nursing home version: A useful tool for behavioral interventions in long term care. *Aging and Mental Health, 13*(3), 445–455.
Miller, J. G. (1964). Psychodivorce: A psychodramatic technique. *Group Psychotherapy, 17,* 129–133.
Miller, J. G., & Brydon-Miller, M. (2004, July 28–August 1). *The navigator as therapist.* Presentation at the American Psychological Association Annual Convention, Honolulu, Hawaii.
Montsaingeon, B. (1985). *Mademoiselle: Conversations with Nadia Boulanger.* Manchester, England: Carcanet.
Neff K. (2003). Development and validation of a scale to measure self-compassion. *Self and Identity, 2,* 223–250.
O'Brien, P. (1976). *Picasso: A biography.* New York: Norton.
Osborn, A. (1957). *Applied imagination: Principles and procedures of creative thinking.* New York: Scribner.
Pennebaker, J. W., Kiecolt-Glaser, J. K., & Glaser, R. (1988). Disclosure of traumas and immune function: Health implications for psychotherapy. *Journal of Consulting and Clinical Psychology, 56*(2), 239–245.
Pennebaker, J. W., & Seagal, J. D. (1999). Forming a story: The health benefits of narrative. *Journal of Clinical Psychology, 55,* 1243–1254.
Pretzer, J. (2004). Cognitive therapy of personality disorders. In J. J. Magnavita (Ed.), *Handbook of personality disorders* (pp. 169–193). New York: Wiley.
Robertson, J., & McDaniel, C. (2000). *Painting as a language: Material technique, form, content.* Belmont, CA: Thompson-Wadsworth.
Rogers, C. (1951). *Client-centered therapy: Its current practice, implications, and theory.* London: Constable.
Roy, K. M., & McAdams, D. P. (2006). Second chances as transformative stories in human development: An introduction. *Research in Human Development, 3*(2&3), 77–80.
Sarbin, T. (Ed.). (1986). *Narrative psychology: The storied nature of human conduct.* New York: Praeger.
Seligman, M. E. P (1998). *Learned optimism: How to change your mind and your life.* New York: Penguin Books. (Original work published 1991)
Seligman, M. E. P. (2002). *Authentic happiness: Using the new positive psychology to realize your potential for lasting fulfillment.* New York: Free Press.
Shapiro, F. (Ed.). (2002). *EMDR as an integrative psychotherapy approach. Experts of diverse orientations exlore the paradigm prism.* Washington, DC: American Psychological Association.
Shapiro F. (Ed.). (2008). *EMDR as an integrative psychotherapy approach: Experts of diverse orientations explore the paradigm prism.* Washington, DC: American Psychological Association.
Sharpe, L., & Gunther, I. (1994). *Editing: Fact and fiction.* Cambridge, England: Cambridge University Press.
Simkin, J. (1975). Gestalt therapy in groups. In G. M. Gazda (Ed.), *Basic approaches to group psychotherapy and group counseling* (2nd ed.). Springfield, IL: Thomas.

Skinner, B. F. (1930). *The behavior of organisms.* New York: Appleton-Century-Crofts.

Smith, J., & Helm, R. (2003). Focused expressive writing as self-help for stress and trauma: KCLP in session. *Psychotherapy in Practice, 59*(2), 227–335.

Smyth, J. M., Stone, A. A., Hurewitz, A., & Kaell, A. (1999, April 14). Effects of writing about stressful experiences on symptom reduction in patients with asthma or rheumatoid arthritis: A randomized trial. *Journal of the American Medical Association, 281*(14), 1289.

Steiner, C. M. (1974). *Scripts people live: Transactional analysis of life scripts.* New York: Bantam.

Strupp, H. H. (1955). An objective comparison of Rogerian and psychoanalytic techniques. *Journal of Consulting Psychology, 19,* 1–7.

Strupp, H. H., Hadley, S. W., & Gomes-Schwartz, B. (1979). Specific vs. non-specific factors in psychotherapy: A controlled outcome study. *Archives of General Psychiatry, 36,* 1125–1136.

Thompson, J. *John Thompson's modern course for the piano: The second grade book.* Cincinnati, OH: The Willis Music Company.

Tucker, P. H. (1989). *Monet in the 90's: The series paintings.* Boston, MA: Museum of Fine Arts.

Vandervoort, H., & McIlvenna, T. M. (n.d.). *You can last longer.* San Francisco, CA: Multi-Media Resource Center.

Van der Kolk, B. (2002). Beyond the talking cure: Somatic experience and subcortical imprints in the treatment of trauma. In F. Shapiro (Ed.), *EMDR as an integrative psychotherapy approach: Experts of diverse orientations explore the paradigm prism* (pp. 85–122). Washington, DC: American Psychological Association.

Vasari, G. (1967). Leonardo da Vinci. In *Lives of the painters, sculptors and architects.* New York: Dutton. (Original work published 1550)

Vedantum, S. (2008, June 23). Social isolation growing in US, study says (para 1). Retrieved May 24, 2012, from http://www.washingtpost.com

Wheat, A., & Larkin, K. (2010). Biofeedback of heart rate variability and related physiology: A critical review. *Applied Psychophysiology and Biofeedback, 35*(3), 229–242.

White, M. (1995). *Re-Authoring lives: Interviews and essays.* Adelaide, Australia: Dulwich Centre.

White, M. J., & Epston, M. (1990). *Narrative means to therapeutic ends.* New York: Norton.

Williams, P., & Davis, D. (2002) *Therapist as life coach: Transforming your practice.* New York: Norton.

Wolpe, J. (1958). *Psychotherapy by reciprocal inhibition.* Stanford, CA: Stanford University Press.

Index